The Ultimate Book of Heroic Failures

Stephen Pile was a journalist for far too long and is the author of *The Book of Heroic Failures*. He is also the Founder and President of the Not Terribly Good Club of Great Britain and was the Artistic Director of the First International Nether Wallop Arts festival in 1984, which came about by accident. The next week Stephen met his wife, had three children, became a television critic for fourteen years and hasn't been out of the house since, which is why Britain looks so strange and changed.

THE
ULTIMATE BOOK *of*
HEROIC FAILURES

STEPHEN PILE

faber and faber

First published in 2011
by Faber and Faber Limited
Bloomsbury House
74–77 Great Russell Street
London WC1B 3DA
This paperback edition first published in 2012

Typeset by Faber and Faber Limited
Printed in England by CPI Group (UK) Ltd, Croydon, CRO 4YY

The right of Stephen Pile to be identified as author
of this work has been asserted in accordance with Section 77
of the Copyright, Designs and Patents Act 1988

A CIP record for this book
is available from the British Library

ISBN 978–0–571–27731–5

2 4 6 8 10 9 7 5 3 1

CONTENTS

'If all else fails, immortality can always be assured
by spectacular error.'

J. K. GALBRAITH

INTRODUCTION

'There is much to be said for failure.
It is more interesting than success.'
MAX BEERBOHM

Success is overrated.

We all crave it despite daily evidence that our real genius lies in exactly the opposite direction. Incompetence is what we are good at. It is what marks us off from the animals. We should learn to revere it. All successful people are the same. You know, drive, will to win, determination . . . it is just too dull to contemplate, whereas everyone who messes up big time does so in a completely individual way. Doing something badly requires skill, panache, genius, exquisite timing and real style.

MY SQUAD

Like a proud Olympic captain, I now stand in the tunnel waiting to lead my squad out into the arena. This is the A-team, the crème de la crème, gods among men, elite practitioners who were so bad in their chosen field that they soar like fireworks across a dull, grey sky. Never before have so many giants been gathered together in the same place. Look-

[1]

ing down the line, I see the all-time greats – here is the atrocious Criswell, the alarming Murrell, the immortal Molina, the disgraceful Stinky Holloway.

The gang's all here.

The crowd hoots and hats are thrown into the air. If I can make myself heard above the din, there is just time to say that we are living in an era of great achievement. This is a golden age. World records have toppled and standards get higher.

We all thought that Pat Farley's record of four hundred driving lessons before passing a test would never be surpassed, but no. Thanks to the illustrious Sue Evan-Jones of Bristol we now realise that four hundred is peanuts and Mrs Farley was barely skimming the surface of what is possible in this area. The record for the most call-outs of a lifeboat on a single voyage has shot up from four to a monumental eleven and Frances Toto has equalled the record for the most attempts to murder a spouse without him noticing that anything was wrong (seven).

Because I take a necessarily international view of all this, I have to tell you that the category devoted to the Most Failed Driving Tests is now closed due to a world-beating Korean called Cha Sa-soon, whose performance is unlikely ever to be surpassed.

The fastest sending-off in a football match is now down to one second and the worst angler did not catch a fish for forty years. After centuries of democracy we at last have the first ever election at which nobody voted at all. The worst racehorse used to be a fine British animal with no competitive instinct whatever, but now he has been entirely outclassed by a very exciting horse from Puerto Rico.

The amazing world of crime continues to astonish (the worst mugger left his victim considerably better off), but the police too have a vitally important role to play.

The worst weather forecast ever led to the suspension of TV weather forecasting until the climate was more reliable, while the least successful sermon caused the church to burn down.

In the world of rugby league Runcorn Highfield are the team to beat, having broken Doncaster's long-standing record for the most successive defeats.

The least successful film ever at the box office was released at the same time as the first *Harry Potter* film and only now can it receive the acclaim that it so thoroughly deserves.

CAN ANYONE DO IT?

This book sings the praises of exceptional people, but do not be disheartened. This is the pinnacle, the top of the pyramid, but these immortals have merely explored a potential that is in each and every one of us. People sometimes ask: 'Could I too be really awful at something?' Well, yes, of course, you could.

You too could live the dream. This is people's

art and open to all. It is perfectly possible to be incompetent for hours on end. I certainly am and so is everyone I know. The marvellous thing is that it can be done in spare moments, even during a lunch break (see the distinguished Matthieu Boya, Chapter 15).

The unparalleled exploits celebrated here come from all corners, from Worthing to Wisconsin, from the Outer Hebrides to the North Pole. There are no national boundaries and no class distinctions. Even the Queen Mother got involved. New territories are also emerging and it is a great pleasure to welcome to the fold Syria, which now holds the all-comers record for the driver who got most lost under satnav direction.

We are also indebted to the great American nation, which affects to be unimpressed by its own achievements in this line, but its genius is second to none. *Moose Murders,* which is the undisputed Worst Ever Broadway Play, is here reconstructed from reviews of the period so we can all now relive the whole magical experience. Furthermore, this pioneering country has also produced the immortal Ed Wood, who is our Shakespeare.

Widely acclaimed as the world's worst film director, he created the template from which the rest of us are fabulous variations. He combined enthusiasm and utter self-belief with a total lack of ability that is only seen once in a generation, if that. The result is that his work backs through badness and out the other side into something so wondrous that it will live forever.

Ability is accidental and this great man shows that it is possible to do astonishing things without any whatsoever. As one critic has pointed out, 'He achieved high art through sheer incompetence.' Mr Wood is the only person, alive or dead, to have three entries in this book. For that reason there is a homage to him in Chapter 9.

IS SPECIAL EQUIPMENT NEEDED?

For this life-enhancing activity you need little equipment. Some have done it with just a family-sized bucket of Kentucky Fried Chicken. Others have needed only a flagpole. That said, horses have historically offered quite spectacular opportunities. The important thing, remember, is to improvise.

You can do it at home or at sea, at work or in a deckchair with helium balloons attached ten thousand feet above Los Angeles. It can be done on stage, in a guesthouse or even standing in a field with two escaped pigs.

OUR WAY OF LIFE IS UNDER THREAT

Like the Masai, our ancestral way of life is under threat. Indeed, it will interest Masai warriors everywhere to learn that in the offshore island of Britain where I live we once had a woman called Margaret Thatcher, whom older people here still remember. In 1980 she made a preposterous speech saying that we are now an island devoted to success, not failure.

That woman has stolen our birthright. Our land is now awash with people who never tire of telling us that they are delivering excellence, whether they are or not. It is now even possible to earn a living in this country as a spin doctor or a public-relations guru telling us that everything is going well when it obviously isn't. These people are actually employed to cover up our mistakes. Why? Whatever for?

We will not be silenced.

REDISCOVERING OUR ROOTS

It is a grave misreading of the human predicament to suppose that everything is going to work out well. Happiness lies in not only accepting that things go belly up, but also rejoicing in them when they do.

For years we have been told that success is the thing, but in Britain, for example, it only took John Sergeant to start dancing for the whole nation to rise up in his support. The sleeping giant awakes. We rediscover our ancient qualities.

This outstanding man (he is our top dancer, quite frankly) could not waltz for nuts and there he was on a perfection-crazed TV dance competition. Week after week the judges condemned his exquisite rumbas and called for his immediate departure. Week after week the viewers voted overwhelmingly to keep him on the show and send home his drably excellent rivals.

It is worth noticing that Maurice Flitcroft, the world's worst golfer, evoked the same response. By the end of his career you could address a letter to 'Maurice Flitcroft, Golfer, England' and it would get there.

It is not just in Britain that this happens. When Eric 'the Eel' Moussambani practically drowned in his Olympic qualifying heat the whole world rose to applaud him. When the Jamaicans entered the Winter Olympics, came last and fell off their bobsleigh, Hollywood were on the phone straight away and made a film about them.

For me this volume is the culmination of a life's work in my area of scholarship. It seems a long time now since I formed the Not Terribly Good Club of Great Britain back in the simpler pre-digital days of 1978 with myself, cocooned in administrative chaos, as president. To qualify for membership you just had to be not terribly good at something and attend meetings at which people talked about and gave demonstrations of their main area of expertise. We had some glorious evenings when you heard snatches of heart-warming conversation ('Yes, sheep are difficult' – Not Terribly Good Artist). Eventually, I was thrown out as president and the club voted itself out of existence when it received several thousand applications for membership, some from as far away as Botswana. This can only be read as yet further proof of humanity's preference for the worst over the best.

We can wait no longer in the tunnel. Outside the vuvuzelas beckon. I now lead out my team. Onward and downward.

☞ 1 ☜

NEW WORLD RECORDS

Brazil's Worst Footballer
The Slowest Cross-Channel Swim
The Worst Ever Broadway Play
The Least Successful Learner Driver
The Worst Rugby League Team
The Most Crowded Bank Robbery
The Most Failed Driving Tests
The Biggest Football Defeat
The Worst Racehorse
The Worst-Selling Film
The Least Successful Show at the
Edinburgh Festival
The Least Successful Gambler
The Least Successful Navigator
The Most Pointless Election
The Heaviest World Cup Defeat
The Fastest Stage Walk-Off
The Least Successful Penalty Shoot-Out
The Fastest Sending-Off
The Worst Tennis Player
The Most Boring Day

'Try again. Fail again. Fail better.'
SAMUEL BECKETT

Brazil's Worst Footballer

Universally acclaimed as the worst professional team ever to have played upon the face of this planet, Ibis of Recife in Brazil did not win a game for three years and eleven months. 'It was a great privilege to have that reputation. It's better than playing for the world's best team,' said their captain, the legendary Mauro Shampoo, who has been hailed as Brazil's worst footballer. 'We even had a fan club in Portugal. When we started to win they sent us angry telegrams.'

A key part of the Ibis strike force, the great man scored one goal in ten years, but his record was otherwise unblemished. His unique and recurrent ability was to fall over the ball when there was no other player near him. 'Because he is such a terrible player,' his daughter said, 'he became famous. And now he's out there.'

He is the subject of a sensitive documentary film called *Mauro Shampoo: Footballer, Hairdresser, Man.* This is how he habitually answers the telephone at his salon, where the walls are covered with memorabilia from his splendid career.

To this day Sr Shampoo, who called his children Cream Rinse and Shampoozinho, has persisted with his Kevin Keegan 1970s permed haircut long after Kevin decided it was the wrong direction. In the salon he is immediately recognisable because he spends the month of December dressed in an unconvincing Father Christmas suit. The rest of the year he wears his Ibis football kit, including studs, so that between haircuts he can give demonstrations of his celebrated ball control to reassure customers that he has lost none of his old touch.

The Slowest Cross-Channel Swim

The fastest swim across the Channel was completed in a hasty six hours and fifty-seven minutes by some frantic Bulgarian, but our sort of swimmer prefers to savour the experience. For seventy-seven years Henry Sullivan's fine record of twenty-seven hours and twenty-five minutes stood unchallenged as the slowest ever. After six earlier attempts when Mr Sullivan was fished out of the water anything up to five miles away from the French coast, he finally completed the swim in August 1923.

His record stood as a glowing example until 2010, when Jackie Cobell of Tonbridge in Kent did it in a splendid twenty-eight hours and forty-four minutes. 'The cliffs of Calais kept disappearing. That's when the tide took me out,' said Mrs Cobell, who lost eight stone as part of her training regime with the aid of a gastric belt.

'I'm always up for a challenge,' she said, 'I wouldn't

mind doing the Alcatraz swim next. They've got sharks there so it might make me go a bit quicker.'

The Worst Ever Broadway Play

An immediate and sensational flop, *Moose Murders* by Arthur Bicknell is now widely considered to be the worst play ever performed on Broadway. 'If your name is Arthur Bicknell – or anything like it – change it,' said the theatre critic at CBS.

When it opened and closed on 22 February 1983, Frank Rich, the drama critic of the *New York Times*, wrote: 'From now on there will always be two groups of theatregoers in this world: those who have seen *Moose Murders* and those who have not. Those of us who have witnessed it will undoubtedly hold periodic reunions in the noble tradition of survivors of the *Titanic*.'

The play, a mystery farce, relates the adventures of Snooks and Howie Keene, Nurse Dagmar, Stinky Holloway and others trapped together one excellent stormy night at the Wild Moose Lodge, a guesthouse in the Adirondack Mountains. Several murders take place, Stinky tries to sleep with his mother and a man in a moose costume is assaulted by a bandage-wrapped quadriplegic.

There is a thunderclap. The curtain rises on a hunting lodge which is attractively festooned with stuffed moose heads.

Act One gets off to a corking start when 'The Singing Keenes', the in-house entertainers, come on and launch straight into a rendition of 'Jeepers Creepers'. A scantily clad Snooks Keene sings in an off-key screech. She is accompanied by her blind husband pounding away on his electric organ until the plug is pulled out by the resident caretaker, Joe Buffalo Dance, who wears Indian war paint but speaks with an Irish brogue.

They are soon joined by the wealthy Hedda Holloway, the Lodge's new owner. She arrives with her husband Sidney, the heavily bandaged quadriplegic, who is confined to a wheelchair. His attendant, Nurse Dagmar, wears revealing black satin, barks like a Nazi and whenever possible leaves her patient out in the rain.

In addition to her son Stinky, a drug-crazed Oedipal hippie, Mrs Holloway has a young daughter called Gay, who is permanently in a party dress. When told that her father will always be a vegetable, she turns up her nose and replies, 'Like a lima bean? Gross me out!' and then breaks into a tap dance.

Just before the interval Stinky gets out a deck of cards to give the actors, if not the audience, something to do. The lights go out mid-game and the first of several inexplicable murders is committed.

'Even Act One of *Moose Murders* is inadequate preparation for Act Two,' Mr Rich wrote. In the play's final twist Mrs Holloway serves Gay a poison-laced vodka Martini for reasons that are never entirely clear. As the young girl collapses to the floor and croaks in the middle of a Shirley Temple tap-dancing routine, her mother breaks into laughter and applause.

The leading lady was supposed to be making her comeback after more than forty years away from the Broadway stage, but she dropped out after the first preview.

To mark the twenty-fifth anniversary of its opening and closing the play was restaged as a conceptual art project. 'Broadway had its chance and they blew it,' the artist said.

The Least Successful Learner Driver

In a highly competitive field we could not expect Pat Farley's achievement to last long. By the time she finally passed her driving test at Ashburton in Devon she was a very experienced driver, having already motored six thousand miles during her four hundred lessons, costing £4,500. In February 1997 this record was comprehensively shattered by the gifted Sue Evan-Jones from Bristol, who took 1,800 lessons and twenty-seven years to pass her test, at a cost of £20,000 including a course of hypnotherapy.

During this fine run she had ten instructors and lost count of the number of times they pleaded with her to stop the car. In that period they only felt confident enough to enter her for a test three times.

In her first test she hit the clutch pedal instead of the brake and ploughed into coned-off roadworks. On her second attempt she pulled out into the path of a police car, which had its sirens on and lights flashing. By the end Nick George, her final driving instructor, had been giving her free lessons four times a week for a year because he regarded her as a challenge.

The Worst Rugby League Team

Setting a new all-time rugby league record, Runcorn Highfield played a mouth-watering seventy-five games without a win between November 1988 and March 1991. For much of this time they were led by their charismatic player-coach, Geoff Fletcher. Nobody knew how old he was, but he used to hang his wig in the changing room before the match.

Scouring Australia for new talent, Runcorn scouts came back with the only one-armed player ever to appear in the rugby league. Once the entire team went on strike and stood in the crowd booing their own side, having asked for an increase in 'losing pay'. The management had only offered to increase their winning pay, which was preposterous in the circumstances. Runcorn fielded a team of reserves plus their new coach, a thirty-nine-year-old born-again Christian who came out of retirement to play and was sent off after eleven minutes for violent conduct. They lost 92–2.

Runcorn easily shattered the existing record of forty matches without a win. This was held by Doncaster, who not only became the first club in any sport to put their entire team up for sale in 1980, but also admitted in a TV documentary that in muddy conditions they did not recognise their own jerseys and often tackled each other. After a streaker had run topless across the pitch before an international match at Twickenham, Doncaster advertised for a woman with a forty-two-inch bust to do likewise at their ground, Tatty's Field, in a final attempt to attract a crowd. 'We would quite happily settle for anything from thirty-eight inches upwards,' the team's manager, Tom Norton, said when there was no immediate response.

The Most Crowded Bank Robbery

In October 1994 awed cashiers in the Paraguayan town of Abai could only watch and learn as their bank became the first ever to be held up by two different gangs of robbers at the same time. The modest amount of cash in the safe that morning was shared equally between them. 'Apparently they gave each other dirty looks as they scampered out the door,' a police spokesman said afterwards.

The Most Failed Driving Tests

Cha Sa-soon of South Korea blazed the trail in 2009 when she failed her driving test a world-beating 959 times. She had failed the test on 771 occasions when she decided to sit it daily.

She took her first written theory section of the test in April 2005 at the Jeonbuk Drivers' Licence Agency of the south-western city of Jeonju. 'What she was doing essentially', an official at the agency said, 'was memorising as many questions and answers as possible without understanding what they were about.'

Things started to look bad when Mrs Cha passed the theory section in November 2009, but there was no need to worry because she then failed the road-skills section four times and the road test four times as well. In honour of her achievement Hyundai gave her a $16,800 car and she now stars in their national prime-time advertising campaign. 'I didn't mind,' said Mrs Cha. 'To me, committing every day to take the test was like going to school. I always missed school.' Her name means 'vehicle' in Korean.

The Biggest Football Defeat

For more than a century the all-important team in world football was Bon Accord, who lost 36–0 in a Scottish league match against Arbroath in 1885. This feat was completely overshadowed in October 2002 when Stade Olympique de L'Emyrne lost 149–0 to their arch rivals AS Adema in a Madagascar national league game. Even more impressively, they were all own goals.

In commanding form Stade Olympique took complete control of the match. No member of the winning team touched the ball between the first goal and the hundred and forty-ninth. From kick-off SOE thumped the ball back to their defenders who whacked it past their own goalkeeper, while the outplayed Adema team stood around looking bemused.

This dominant performance was masterminded from the stands by the SOE coach in protest over refereeing decisions that had gone against them in an earlier match.

The Worst Racehorse

The all-conquering Quixall Crossett became the world's least successful racehorse in 1998 when he lost an impressive 103 races in a row. He was described by the *Racing Post* as 'a seriously slow horse that is in danger of becoming a folk hero'.

According to his breeder, Ted Caine: 'I've put him in some of the worst races there are. He hasn't got an engine as such, but he enjoys jumping around.' Quixall Crossett was eventually retired after pressure from the Jockey Club, which was reluctant to renew his permit, noting that he was showing 'receding interest in getting competitive on the racecourse'.

The previous worst was Amrullah, who entered seventy-four races without victory. He had his own fan club and his retirement was announced on the *BBC News at 10*.

British horses are not what they were, sadly, and the competitive edge has now passed to an exciting Puerto Rican animal called Doña Chepa. To commemorate Doña's 125th loss in a row at Camarero racetrack in 2007 her trainer, Efrain Nieves, was presented with a plaque.

The Worst-Selling Film

January 2006 is mistakenly remembered as the launch date of *Harry Potter and the Never-Ending Sequels*. Sadly, it drew attention away from *Offending Angels*, which was released in the same week and became the worst-selling film in British cinema history.

This film had everything. There was a fabulous plot about two laddish, layabout housemates who occasionally go outside to play cricket. God takes pity on them and sends a pair of guardian angels, Zeke and Paris, to lead them back to a life of virtue and industry. Happily, Paris used to be a dolphin and Zeke was formerly a squirrel so divine intervention proves a bit of a mixed blessing. Eventually they all fall in love.

Just days before the filming was due to begin, the Indian hotelier who had agreed to fund half the budget sent a one-line fax saying the deal was off. The print of the film and the sound mix were both lost twice in the confusion which followed.

It certainly provoked a reaction from the critics, which is what you always hope for. The *Guardian* said: 'The direction is out to lunch and the script is four drafts away from anything usable,' while *Total Film* said: 'To be fair, there is one mildly amusing scene in a Chinese restaurant, but it is the pastoral sex scene and the wet-eyed finale that live in the memory.'

At a cinema in Croydon the only people who saw the film all week were the projectionist and the usher. Fewer than twenty people around the UK paid to see it. After VAT and the cinemas' cut, it made a total profit at the box office of £17. When the DVD came out, it became a cult collector's item and an opportunity to own a piece of cinema history. 'It might even double my takings,' said the indomitable director.

The Least Successful Show at the Edinburgh Festival

Living up to its name, The Empty Space Theatre Company set a new record at the Edinburgh Festival in 1988 when not one person turned up to see its show. Company members handed out dozens of complimentary tickets in an attempt to rustle up an audience, but even then people stayed away.

Promising 'A Parable of the Blind', the evocative blurb read: 'Blind, blissful, medieval figures dance towards Brueghel's inevitable ditch, while in a mythical East goldfish have their eyes plucked out in order to sing better.' The group's manager, Miss Amanda McClellan, admitted that if she had read that even she would not have gone to see it.

Mr Gerald Purfield, who had a very quiet time in the box office, said that two people with complimentary tickets did turn up one night, but they were ushered into the wrong show.

The Least Successful Gambler

Mr Mick Bates of Wellington in Shropshire won the acclaim of national newspapers in August 1996 when it emerged that in his entire gambling career he had not won a single bet. His glory days began when he first tried betting on the dogs, only to see his chosen hound stop to urinate. Eventually he switched to the horses, but put money on one that dropped dead during the race.

Turning his attention to athletics, he backed the normally reliable Linford Christie in the 100 metres, who was disqualified after two false starts. He next put money on the triple jump when Jonathan Edwards was having his only off day in years. 'I just seem to put a jinx on everything I back,' said Mr Bates, who now took an interest in football. 'I was so sure England would do badly in the European Championships that I backed their opponents in every match.' He watched as Scotland, Holland and Spain lost.

When England beat Germany in extra time, he went to collect his winnings only to be told that for betting purposes it is the score at ninety minutes that counts.

Eventually he decided to use his great gift for his country's good. To help Tim Henman and Neil Broad win a gold medal for Britain in their Olympic doubles tennis match in 1996 he backed their opponents. With Mr Bates cheering them on, and for once not wanting to win his bet, Henman and Broad were thrashed. In this way our greatest living gambler ended his outstanding run.

The Least Successful Navigator

The existing record for the most call-outs of a lifeboat by a lone sailor used to be four. This was trounced in the summer of 2000 when Eric 'the Navigator' Abbott called out the lifeboat services a triumphant eleven times while cruising in the Irish Sea. A fifty-six-year-old unemployed house painter,

Mr Abbott first set sail in his home-made yacht in July 1999, blaming an unfair taxation system that had forced him out to sea 'to find himself'.

Luckily, his only means of navigation was an AA road map, which is why he was never able to give rescuers even a rough approximation of where he was. Phoning the emergency services, he told them, 'I can see mountains,' or 'I am near a light.'

His world-beating eleventh rescue came when he made a spontaneous unscheduled landing in full view of the commodore of the Rhyl Yacht Club, which had just given him temporary membership. 'I don't think we've ever had a guy this bad,' the commodore said.

When their most regular customer radioed for advice, Holyhead coastguards recognised his voice immediately and wasted no time in launching both inshore and offshore lifeboats. Despite their efforts to divert him, Mr Abbott still missed the river channel into the harbour. 'I was spot-on with my map readings. It was just coming into the harbour that went wrong.'

At the family home in Northwich, Cheshire, his daughter Julie told reporters: 'My dad doesn't have to prove himself to anyone.' Eventually he agreed to go on a ten-day sailing course offered free of charge by the Royal Yachting Association, which brought his glorious career to an unfortunate end.

The Most Pointless Election

Since the dawn of democracy we have waited for the definitive election in which no candidate polled any votes at all. It finally happened when Pillsbury in North Dakota held a council election on 10 June 2008 at which no one voted, not even the people at the ballot station. It is the first time that six candidates have stood unopposed and not one of them has got in.

'Everybody has got a job and they're busy,' said the mayor of this small rural community, Darrel Brudevold, who was going to vote for himself, but had crops to tend. The mayor's wife is the postmistress and also runs a beauty shop so she too was rushed off her feet.

The council meets about five times a year. 'Members are each paid $48 annually and a good portion of that goes on doughnuts for the meeting,' the mayor said.

The county auditor told the councillors to appoint someone to do their jobs, so they appointed themselves.

The Heaviest World Cup Defeat

The Maldives graced the World Cup for the first time ever in 1997. To a competition that was often marked by defensive, tactical play they brought a breath of fresh air. Every game in which they played was guaranteed to be a goal feast.

They played a key role, for example, in every single goal when Iran beat them 17–0, setting a new record. Consistency is a byword with the Maldives because they lost 12–0 to Syria twice.

After the Iran match half the Maldives team went to their coach, Romulo Cortez, and said they wanted to give up football. It took some time to dissuade them. In the whole of the World Cup they did nothing so self-centred as score a goal.

Dwarfing the Maldives' achievement in a qualifying match for the 2002 World Cup, however, American Samoa lost to Australia 31–0. The coach sought divine intervention before the game. '"Frightened" is not the word,' he said. 'We are asking the Lord to help keep the score down.' There were so many goals that even the scoreboard operator got confused and FIFA had to confirm the result with the referee.

The Fastest Stage Walk-Off

For a quarter of a century the great actor Alan Devlin was unsurpassed in his ability to leave the stage long before the play had ended. Three times he showed his mastery of the premature exit, and his most memorable performance came in the 1987 production of *HMS Pinafore* at the Gaiety

Theatre in Dublin. He had delivered half his lines when he turned to the audience, said 'F—— this for a game of soldiers. I'm going home,' and clambered through the orchestra pit shouting, 'Finish it yourself.'

Really great actors live on in the mind long after they have left the stage and Mr Devlin was no exception. Still wired for sound, he could be heard ordering a round of drinks in the pub next door.

All his great departures occurred halfway through a production to give the audience some idea how dull the evening would be without his intervention. In January 1998, however, he met his match when the immortal Adrian Hood gave the performance of a lifetime at the West Yorkshire Playhouse and, setting a new world record, walked off after the first line of John Godber's *Weekend Break*.

Playing the part of a stand-up comedian afflicted by anxiety, our man walked into the spotlight, said, 'I hate flying I do', and left the stage for the rest of the evening. Oh, he was good. He was very good. Cutting straight through to the heart of this role, he conveyed the wordless essence of anxiety through a perfectly executed panic attack.

The playwright himself read the part from there on. John Sully, of Leeds City Council, who was in the audience, said: 'The audience seemed to enjoy it very much. It made for a unique evening.'

People rushing to the theatre next night were disappointed to find that Mr Hood was word-perfect.

The Least Successful Penalty Shoot-Out

Penalty shoot-outs are an impatient modern idea to get football games over and done with instead of enjoying the sheer pleasure of replaying the match. Only Mickleover Lightning Blue Sox and Chellaston Boys have done it properly in the longest and most satisfying penalty shoot-out in football history.

After a 1–1 draw in a 1988 Derby Community Cup match, they missed the first sixty-two penalty kicks. This was a feast of spectacular football entertainment that gave real value for money and showcased their full repertoire, scuffing, muffing, blasting and ballooning balls skilfully over the bar.

Then a boy called Richard Smith scored for Chellaston. This regrettable event only fired up the other team and John Blatherwick equalised for Mickleover. Chellaston valiantly missed the next shot, but it was downhill from here on. Sam Gadsby, about whom the less said the better, spoiled everything by scoring the winner.

At ninety minutes this is the first ever penalty shoot-out to last as long as the match.

The Fastest Sending-Off

The days are long gone when Giuseppe Lorenzo led the world. Playing for Bologna, he was sent off after a leisurely ten seconds. To show that our modern world is getting faster Lee Todd was shown a red card after just two seconds in a Sunday league match against Taunton East Reach Wanderers. When the referee blew his whistle for kick-off, Mr Todd said, 'F—— me, that was loud,' and got sent off.

This was not the fastest, however, because that all-time great, the awesome Chris Glanville, was brought on as a substitute for Deanwood in the Medway Sunday League in December 1996. He was sent off after one second for wearing an ear stud, having put only one foot on the pitch.

'The referee told him to take the stud out, but he couldn't. He'd only just had it pierced,' said John Wren, the secretary of Deanwood. 'He was one of our younger second-team players and our manager just wanted to give him a little run out.' That mission was very much accomplished.

Even this is not the record, which is jointly held by Keith Gillespie of Sheffield United and Walter Boyd of Swansea City. In separate matches they both ran onto the pitch, immediately lamped an opponent and were sent off. On both occasions the ball was out of play so they were technically dismissed after nought seconds.

The Worst Tennis Player

Diego Beltranena became the world's most important tennis player in August 2005 when he lost an epic fifty-four international matches in a row, winning only one set. The great Guatemalan's world record was bettered in only three years, however.

By 2008 Britain's own Robert Dee had lost fifty-four international matches in a row but without winning a single set. Disappointingly he missed the chance to break the world record outright when he cracked under pressure and won his fifty-fifth match.

A British newspaper did award Mr Dee the ultimate accolade of 'The World's Worst Tennis Player', but incredibly he declined this compliment and took them to court. In fact, the judge reassured him that he was without question the world's worst until overtaken, although he is clearly unworthy of the title with such an inexplicable attitude problem.

The Most Boring Day

Feeding three hundred million facts into a specially designed search engine, the British researcher William Tunstall-Pedoe found that 11 April 1954 was officially the dullest day of the twentieth century. On this day of days almost nothing happened. There were no coups, no crashes, no monkeys in space. The Oldham Athletic footballer Jack Shuffle-botham passed away at the age of sixty-nine and there was a peaceful election in Belgium. It was also the birthday of the electrical engineer Abdullah Atalar, whose later research interests included 'integrated circuit design and the linearisation of RF power amplifiers'.

There were apparently plans for a *coup d'état* in Yanaon, a one-time French colony in India, but this did not actually materialise. Dogs slept, cows were milked, and children skipped and grew.

2

TAKING THE INITIATIVE

The Least Successful Survival Talk
The Worst War Correspondent
The Least Successful Prosecution Counsel
The Worst Polar Expedition
The Least Successful Elvis Impersonator
The Least Successful Literary Pilgrimage
The Most Over-Enthusiastic Armed Response
The Worst Official Bridge Opening
The Least Successful Disguise I
The Least Successful Disguise II
The Least Successful Mugger
The Worst Criminal Partnership I
The Worst Criminal Partnership II
The Least Successful Citizen's Arrest
Bomb Disposal News
The Least Successful Safe Sex Campaign
The Least Convincing Campaign Group

'A real failure does not need an excuse.
It is an end in itself.'

GERTRUDE STEIN

The Least Successful Survival Talk

Invited to give a lecture on how to survive in the wild, Alistair Emms arrived early at Allhallows School, which is perched on remote cliff tops near Seaton in Devon. Having time to spare on that fine day in October 1992, he decided to go for a stroll before delivering his talk. When he had not returned an hour later coastguards were sent off to search for him.

Finding no trace, they called in the police and two other coastguard units. By this stage forty local people, five police officers, a tracker dog and two helicopters were involved. It took five hours to rescue the intrepid Mr Emms.

Jeremy Willis, the school's head of music, said: 'One team scaled the cliff face, cutting through bushes, and eventually found him.' Mr Emms was winched onto the helicopter. The lecture was never delivered.

The Worst War Correspondent

The greatest living war correspondent in our field is Phesheya Dube, who was 'Our Man in Baghdad' for Radio Swaziland's breakfast show in March 2003. He sent vivid, breathless eyewitness reports from the Iraq war. These became all the more impressive when it was discovered that he was, in fact, broadcasting from a broom cupboard in Mbabane, the Swazi capital.

In the confusion of war it is often difficult to get accurate facts, but it appears that Mr Dube cobbled together his stories from reports on TV and may even have had access to sound effects. The studio presenter frequently expressed concerns about his safety. He once urged him to find a cave to hide from missiles. When the radio station briefly lost contact with our man, the presenter asked listeners to pray for him.

War reporters who were actually in Iraq took days to travel from one end of the country to the other, but Mr Dube could skip from Baghdad to Basra with remarkable ease and very little expense. Such was the stress of life in a war zone that he popped out for the occasional stroll around Mbabane. Once when he was passing the parliament building, MPs rushed out to congratulate him on his vivid reportage and begged him not to go back. When they heard him broadcasting later that afternoon, questions were asked in parliament.

Great radio of this sort conjures up entire worlds in our imagination. The whole of Radio 4 could be coming from a broom cupboard for all we know.

The Least Successful Prosecution Counsel

Few lawyers have proved themselves more able to outwit their opponents than Sir Harold Cassel. His greatest performance came at Bow Street Magistrates' Court in the 1950s. He was prosecuting a man accused of stealing a motorcycle and had made a pretty convincing case when he discovered that this fellow had no one to defend him. Offering his own services, he stepped in, destroyed his own arguments and got the man off. When the case finished the magistrate said that 'both counsels had been most helpful'.

In later life Sir Harold became an equally distinguished judge. Addressing two defendants who appeared before him on a charge of stealing cigarette lighters, he said: 'You are fortunate that you come up before the worst criminal judge in England.'

Once, when trying a man who claimed to have been injured by police handcuffs, he ignored loud police protestations and tested the handcuffs on himself. 'Now then, officer,' he said eventually. 'Perhaps you'd care to take these off.' 'But, your honour,' said the policeman, 'I've been trying to tell you that we don't have the key.' Sir Harold cheerfully ate his lunch in handcuffs while the officers hunted high and low for it.

The Worst Polar Expedition

Top explorers are all people of enormous determination. They have self-reliance and a refusal to
give up when others say their goal is impossible.
Led by the immortal José María Molina, the members of the great Spanish North Pole expedition of
1982 had all these qualities in abundance.

In that year four friends decided to mount a
polar expedition after a successful skiing trip to
the Andes. Figuring that the Andes and the North
Pole were probably not that different, they first had
to choose the ideal method of transport. Should it
be huskies, snowmobiles or motorbikes? Obviously
it was motorbikes, even if this did mean carrying
350 litres of gasoline with them. Endlessly inventive, they also designed their own sleds, which were
like three-storey shopping trolleys on skis.

They did not seek expert advice and shrewdly
ignored it when offered. Only when it was pointed
out that they would encounter gaping crevasses,
plunging ravines and the occasional yawning abyss,
did they make their only concession to expert opinion. They packed an enormous two-part bridge.

The governor's office at Svalbard in Norway told
them that going to the North Pole on motorbikes
in a howling wind, particularly with three-storey
shopping trolleys, was hopeless. The office assumed
this had dissuaded them. Next thing the governor

got a phone call saying the expedition had arrived at the airport.

On 26 February 1982 they disembarked with a journalist and a photographer, because you definitely want to record an expedition like this. Almost the entire population of Svalbard went out to the airport to see their equipment being unloaded. They found that the expedition's food was packed not in the usual plastic bags, but in large cardboard boxes from which the bottoms fell out when they got wet on the ice. Their bridge drew admiring gasps and a large crowd looked on as they tried to test their equipment in the car park. The motorbikes could not move the sleds at all when fully loaded. When unloaded and given a helping push, they fell over.

Eventually the explorers decided that snowmobiles would be better after all. They tried to sell their motorbikes, but nobody wanted to buy them.

Due to delays the ice melted around Svalbard and the expedition had to be abandoned. Asked by reporters if they ever got tired of people smiling and shaking their heads at them, our men replied: 'No, we think it is nice having happy people around us.'

The Least Successful Elvis Impersonator

Lil Thompson's Steakhouse in Tennessee held the ultimate Elvis Presley impersonator contest when that singer was at the height of his fame. A large crowd arrived, including Elvis Presley himself, who decided to take part and sat quietly at the back. 'I'm going to mash this,' he said confidently.

Lil was worried the place would go crazy when everyone realised it was Elvis. There was no need. He sang 'Love Me Tender' to polite applause and came third.

The Least Successful Literary Pilgrimage

Being an avid fan of Rupert Brooke's poem 'The Old Vicarage, Grantchester', the Reverend Roy Briggs decided to photograph the famous clock described in the poem with its hands at ten to three:

> Stands the Church clock at ten to three?
> And is there honey still for tea?

In April 1993 he travelled six thousand miles from his parish in Johannesburg to Cambridgeshire, arrived at Grantchester just in time, found the house, went into the garden and got out his camera. The clock had stopped at five past one.

The Most Over-Enthusiastic Armed Response

In March 1998, police squad cars roared into Rolvenden with sirens wailing and blue lights flashing. In a faultless demonstration of rapid response they powered manfully into this tranquil Kentish village after a gun was seen being fired from a cottage window.

More than thirty armed officers surrounded the cottage and the village was sealed off for two hours as police waited for the suspect to emerge. Marksmen trained automatic rifles on the building and a negotiator crouched behind a car shouting through a loudhailer: 'We have you surrounded. Come out with your hands in the air.'

Inside, eighty-six-year-old Violet Hook, who was hard of hearing, made herself a pot of tea and relaxed in her kitchen chair, oblivious to the drama. Eventually she heard one of the calls and came out, still carrying the cap gun she used to scare rooks from her roof and demanding to know what all the fuss was about.

Eric Lovell, a friend and neighbour of Mrs Hook, said: 'There were police everywhere pointing their guns at Vi's house. I tried to tell them it was a cap gun, but they ordered me back inside for my own safety.'

When the police screamed at Mrs Hook to throw down her gun, she replied: 'I won't. I don't even know you. And besides I'm going out and I am busy getting ready.'

The Worst Official Bridge Opening

In 1932 a large crowd had formed to see the Premier of New South Wales open a new bridge. He was moments away and the band was playing, flags were waving and the crowd was cheering. Seizing his chance, Francis de Groot, an Irishman on horseback, galloped forward with a sword, shouted, 'In the name of the people of New South Wales I declare this bridge open,' cut the ribbon and galloped off on the other side.

When the Premier arrived he found that it was strangely quiet and the bridge was already open, which was a blessing really because he was a very busy man with many better things he could have been doing. It took some time to catch Mr de Groot but when he was eventually apprehended, he was carted off to a lunatic asylum. After a day-long examination several doctors decided that he was completely sane. He was fined £4 for disturbing the peace and £2 for damaging a ribbon.

The Least Successful Disguise I

In September 1999 police arrested a woman in Los Angeles who was stark naked with a bucket on her head. Asked to explain this promising state of affairs, she said that, while undressed, she had stepped briefly out onto her balcony and the door had locked behind her. Thinking laterally, she put the bucket on her head to hide her identity, went for help and got lost. Not everyone could do that.

The Least Successful Disguise II

One of the finest examples of transparency in policing matters involved PC Dean Cunnington of Albany police station in central London, who in 1997 had a brainwave.

When officers were unable to execute a search warrant on a building to which the only entrance was a closed steel door, PC Cunnington showed himself to be a master of disguise. With a brilliance upon which the Scarlet Pimpernel would struggle to improve, he decided to borrow a postman's outfit.

Now dressed as a postman, he strode up to the door and knocked hard. 'Who is it?' called a voice from within. 'It's the police,' said Constable Cunnington.

The Least Successful Mugger

In March 1993 a mugger approached Roger Morse of Winnipeg, Canada, and shouted, 'Give me your wallet.' Thus far it was a completely traditional mugging transaction in which the mugger stole twenty Canadian dollars. What was much less traditional was that Mr Morse himself next shouted 'Give me my wallet back' to the mugger. We were now entering uncharted and highly experimental waters. Stunned by this unorthodox request, the mugger handed over his own wallet by mistake and fled the scene of the crime, leaving his victim $250 better off.

The Worst Criminal Partnership I

Michael Smith's short but inspirational career in crime came to an abrupt end in June 1995 when his accomplice changed his mind and arrested him. Mr Smith had just pocketed £760, snatched from an employee of William Hill's betting shop in Whitechapel, east London, when his partner in the hold-up put him in a headlock and kept him there until police arrived. 'He had a change of heart,' his solicitor told the court later.

The Worst Criminal Partnership II

Robbing a Detroit record store in December 1994, Clive Robertson shouted, 'Don't anybody move.' When his accomplice reached for the money bag, Mr Robertson shot him in the foot.

The Least Successful Citizen's Arrest

On a sunny October morning in 1995 a young man was lurking suspiciously outside a Dublin branch of the Allied Irish Bank when a security guard walked out with a case full of money.

Suddenly the young man shouted, pulled out a gun, shot the guard, seized the money and leapt onto a getaway motorbike that roared up driven by his accomplice.

As they veered off into the traffic, only one man acted: our hero. A passing van driver saw the whole thing and reversed his Renault into the escaping motorbike. The two villains were thrown onto the bonnet of a nearby car. They stood up and stared at the van driver, aghast and disbelieving.

Aghast and disbelieving also were the director, the sound man, the cameraman and everyone connected with *Crimeline*, the hugely popular Irish TV programme, which was reconstructing an earlier robbery to help police solve it. 'Sometimes it's better,' the *Irish Times* concluded, 'not to get involved.'

Bomb Disposal News

In the winter of 1992 a suspicious-looking package was found outside a Territorial Army centre in Bristol. The TA called the police, who called an army disposal unit, which blew it up. The package was later found to contain leaflets explaining how to correctly identify suspicious-looking packages.

The Least Successful Safe Sex Campaign

In February 1999 the marketing manager of the Society for Family Health in Johannesburg, David Nowitz, admitted that their recent Safe Sex campaign had dramatically increased the danger of sexually transmitted diseases and unwanted pregnancy.

In association with the government they had distributed thousands of pamphlets in Zulu, Xhosa, English, Sotho and Afrikaans, all featuring their character 'Johnny the Condom' and warning against unprotected sex. A free government condom was attached.

'We made a deal with a low-budget distribution company,' Mr Nowitz said, explaining that all the condoms had been perforated when stapled to the leaflet.

The Least Convincing Campaign Group

Fathers 4 Justice was a direct action group set up to argue that divorced fathers were sufficiently responsible to have equal child custody rights with mothers. Speaking after three members had been arrested scaling the gates of Downing Street dressed as Batman to flour-bomb the prime minister, its founder, Matt O'Connor, announced in 2006 that he was closing down the organisation.

'My view is that fathers are not ready for the changes that we want to see,' he said, having concluded that mothers were simply more mature.

Over a three-year period members of Fathers 4 Justice sprayed purple paint over the headquarters of family court officials and caused a forty-minute traffic jam when one of them sat on a 150-foot crane dressed in a Spiderman outfit. They also handcuffed themselves to the children's minister, Mrs Margaret Hodge, at a Law Society conference, announced their intention to kidnap the prime minister's five-year-old son and sat for three days on the roof of the Royal Courts of Justice.

'The truth is that our organisation has been run by women for years,' added Mr O'Connor, who had nothing but praise for their administrative abilities.

☞ 3 ☜

DOING IT IN THE WORKPLACE

Getting the Job Done

The Most Over-Vigilant Security Guard
The Worst Harbour Pilot
The Least Successful Celebration
The Art of Customer Care
The Least Successful Firemen
The Least Satisfactory Lawsuit
The Least Dignified Response to a Job Rejection

The Entrepreneurial Spirit

The Worst Newspaper Proprietor
The Worst Shopping Experience
A Museum Well Worth Visiting
The Worst Pub
The Least Successful Aftershave
The Least Successful Marketing Ploy
The Least Successful Freelance Commission
The Worst Restaurant Name
The Least Successful Promotional Offer
The Worst Timetable
The Least Successful Committee Meeting

'If you're forty years old and have never had a
failure, you've been deprived.'

GLORIA SWANSON

The Most Over-Vigilant Security Guard

The top man in this class is Carl Shimmin, who in May 1991 refused to let the Queen of England into the Royal Windsor Horse Show. 'Sorry, love, you can't come in without a sticker,' he told the monarch, holding up a hand to stop the black Vauxhall Carlton that she had driven herself for the five-hundred-yard journey from Windsor Castle.

'I thought she was an old dear who'd got lost,' he said afterwards, explaining that, as you well know, stickers matter and it was his job to check them. Opening the window, the Queen said: 'I think if you check I will be allowed to come in.'

'The Queen did not seem at all upset,' he observed later. Everyone in her car was smiling happily because it is not every day that you get to meet a true original of this calibre.

The Worst Harbour Pilot

Correctly spotting his vocation, William Lee Murrell became a harbour pilot in March 1860 at

Melbourne's Port Phillip Bay.

Piloting the steamship *Barwon*, he showed early flair when he collided with two other vessels. Clearly this was no fluke. Piloting the SS *Balclutha* a year later, he collided with two more ships, sinking the SS *Aphrasia* and running aground the SS *Minna*.

It was a promising start, but even so no one had any idea of what was to come until 1864 when he was put in charge of piloting the *Southern Cross*, a brand-new steamship, which always seemed to bring out the best in him. Whilst turning this ship around, he destroyed the entire Queen's Wharf. Only a year later he crashed the same ship into the same wharf, which had just been rebuilt.

Showing his versatility, he switched briefly to the *Alhambra* and, while turning that around, crashed into the side of the *Southern Cross*.

It was only now that his true genius started to emerge. Reunited with the *Southern Cross*, he promptly ripped off her propellers in a collision. Two years later he grounded the *Alhambra*. Then he ran the *Macedon* into the *Catherine Jane* and then the *Blackhawk* into the stern of the *Sir Harry Smith*. It is worth mentioning that while manoeuvring the *Dandenong*, he also smashed into the side of the *Alhambra*, completing a personal hat trick with that vessel.

Awed seamen looked on as Mr Murrell now entered his prolific mature period. He ran the *Leura* aground two days running and on the third day, while docking the *Tamar*, he crashed into the side of the *Leura*. Six days later he grounded the *Lady Darling* and then, while docking the *Ringa-rooma*, he ripped off her propeller – twice in two months. Then he crashed the *Omeo* into the *Tamar*, grounded the *Easby* and the *Adela*, again crashed the *Leura* and six months later ran her aground again. Two weeks later he ripped the propeller off the *Mangana*, smashed a wharf with the *Rodondo* and put the *Southern Cross* out of action for a record fifth time.

When this unique matelot retired in 1892 his place in maritime history was assured.

The Least Successful Celebration

Wishing to celebrate High Marnham power station's hundredth accident-free day after a successful safety campaign in 1987, its manager, Mike Johnson, ordered an official flag to be flown. The security guard was hoisting the flag in when a pulley wheel fell off and knocked him out. 'It's true. We boobed,' Mr Johnson said afterwards.

The Art of Customer Care

Giving a masterclass in how to run an orderly hotel, Herr Erwin Wagner put the Pension Kaiser-blick in Sol on the map. Wishing to ensure that his guests got enough rest during their Austrian sojourn in May 1994, he ordered them all to go to bed at 9 p.m.

Edna King, a retired schoolmistress from Leamington Spa, who pointed out that the guests, a group of British tourists, were all middle-aged and completely peaceable, said: 'He stomped in and shouted, "Nine o'clock – finish. You have finished. Go to your rooms." He was banging on the tables and his eyes were popping out of his head. We could not believe it.'

Because they were tired by their long journey, the guests did not argue and went to bed. Next day they were thoroughly refreshed and determined to stay up.

On the second night the diligent Herr Wagner once again demanded that his guests go to bed at nine o'clock. When they refused, he locked them in the dining room and called the police.

One holidaymaker tried to intervene to end the row. With great finesse the owner unhinged one of the doors, then charged after the guests with the door in front of him, chasing them into their rooms.

'We said we did not want to go to bed so early and Herr Wagner flipped,' said Miss King. 'He said we were rowdy, but I only drink lemonade and tea.'

Challenged by the tour operator, Herr Wagner said: 'This is my hotel. If I say it is nine o'clock it is

nine o'clock. We do not have any room for sitting
and talking. I know the English. They drink gin and
whisky when I have gone to bed.'

The Least Successful Firemen

Spotting a small carpet fire in an upstairs bedroom
in her Virginia home in March 2000, Cecilia Perry
called the fire brigade. While waiting, she doused
the flames with buckets of water, helped by neighbours. By the time two fire engines turned up from
rival stations the fire was out.

Still wishing to do brave and manly things, they
both marched into the house and doused the carpet again until a fight broke out as to whose fire call
this was.

During a prolonged dispute the firefighters
smashed furniture and flung each other around the
lower floor of the townhouse. Captain Chauncey
Bowers, a spokesman for the fire department, said
that 'the fire caused about $1,500 worth of damage
and the firemen caused about $3,000'.

The Least Satisfactory Lawsuit

Mustafa Yildirim filed a land ownership case in
1939 claiming that a small plot in western Turkey
belonged to his clients and not to neighbouring
villagers. He was understandably pleased when the

Court of Appeal ruled in favour of his clients fifty-nine years later.

'I was fated to finish this case,' Mr Yildirim told the Anatolian news agency in June 1998. Afterwards he pointed out that he would have to celebrate on his own, because none of his six colleagues involved in the case, nor the fifteen judges who had previously heard it, nor his clients, nor any of the villagers with an interest in the case, whether as plaintiffs or defendants, were still alive, including anyone who could pay his fee.

The Least Dignified Response to a Job Rejection

Being turned down after a job interview is a natural and everyday part of life, as is being sacked, getting laid off or receiving a final warning. How you respond to this is the important thing and Larry Walters set a new high standard in 1982 when his application to become a pilot in the US Air Force was unsuccessful.

Wishing to prove them wrong, he did the only thing possible in the circumstances. He bought forty-five army-surplus weather balloons, filled them with helium and tied them to his garden chair, in which he sat armed with an airgun (to shoot the balloons when he wanted to descend). Instead of rising gently into the air as he had intended, he shot up to a height of eleven thousand feet and into the main approach corridor of Los Angeles airport.

Asked by the helicopter rescue team who hauled him back to earth fourteen hours later on the end of a rope why he had done this, Mr Walters replied: 'A man can't just sit around.'

THE ENTREPRENEURIAL SPIRIT

The Worst Newspaper Proprietor

Proprietors buy newspapers because they like having influence and a team of cowed journalists to do their bidding. In an exciting break with tradition in March 1993, journalists on the *New York Post* greeted their new owner with a front-page headline which screamed: 'Who Is This Nut?'

The paper's popular editor had been sacked on day one, which is par for the course, leaving journalists in the newsroom to their own devices. On the front page there was a portrait of the paper's founder, Alexander Hamilton, digitally embellished with tears in his eyes. Inside, the entire news section was devoted to attacks by staff on the shortcomings of the new owner, Abe 'The Car Park King' Hirschfeld.

In ten pages of withering reportage they alleged that he had once locked a New York City official in her office until she gave him a clean air certificate for one of his car parks. They also pointed out that he had not only compared himself to Einstein and God, but also tried to sack seventy-one of the paper's staff, who had rebelled against his plan to use the paper as a vehicle for his wife's poetry.

Admitting that he knew nothing about newspapers, Mr Hirschfeld said he had given thought to closing the place down and turning it into another car park. The next day's paper had a front-page photo of Mr Hirschfeld next to a headline reading: 'Get Lost!'

All five hundred thousand copies of the paper sold out and it is now a collector's item. Even the boss was pleased. 'It's exactly how I planned,' he said. 'I don't think anybody in history has had ten pages in the *New York Post*. Rome wasn't burnt in a day.'

The Worst Shopping Experience

Few have done as much to stem our unhealthy interest in shopping as Sohan Singh, who made retail history in January 1998 when he became the first ever shopkeeper to ban all his customers from his shop. 'They are rude and noisy,' he explained.

Mr Singh, who described himself as 'a man of principles', had already banned prams, pets, smokers and those who use vulgar language, when he decided that the only way to stem the rising tide of unruly behaviour was to ban the lot of them.

Anyone who wanted to purchase supplies from his Glenthorpe Stores in the Burmantofts district of Leeds was now required to peer through the shop window, decide what they wanted and then ring a bell to be served through a small hatch in the front door.

'It's unbelievable,' said Kathryn Little, who lived opposite. 'He does not get a lot of customers anyway.'

A Museum Well Worth Visiting

If you only visit one museum in your life, make sure it is Louis Tussaud's House of Wax in Great Yarmouth. In 2003 it was hailed by the *Daily Mirror* as 'the worst, and we mean worst, museum in the world'. This is very high praise indeed, but it does have so much to offer.

At Madame Tussaud's in London, which was founded by Louis's more celebrated grandmother, celebrities sit for hours encased in plaster so their brand and image can be paraded before long queues of tourists. The good news is that celebrities are much less willing to go to Great Yarmouth for this purpose and so the waxworks are made from photographs or perhaps even from memory.

The happy result is 150 magnificent waxworks of celebrities, royals, politicians and sportsmen that bear little, if any, resemblance to the people they are meant to represent. Most have name tags which are usually necessary for a confident identification.

Prince Charles has a wild and bushy thatch of uncombed hair and the Irish footballer George Best is often confused with Dustin Hoffman when young. Diana Dors, the blonde-bombshell actress from the 1950s, looks rather homely and has yellow teeth, while Princess Diana has been likened to 'a straw coloured moptop that could be a Saturday afternoon wrestler from the 1970s'. All are dressed in clothes which have about them a pleasant air of Marks & Spencer.

Peter Hayes, now in his eighties, has run this fine museum for more than fifty years. 'There are some very nice ones and I would say Princess Diana is the prize of the collection.'

Outside a sign says: 'These waxworks are best enjoyed as snapshots in time.' Thanks to a charming lack of updating, these wonderful figures are all from the 1970s and early 1980s. It is so much more than just a waxworks. It is a work of art, a time capsule and an urgent lesson on the transience of fame. Who was Sam Fox? Who was Max Boyce?

In a worrying sop to modernisation in 2008, they put seventy waxwork heads up for auction because they were no longer on show. Even Mr Hayes and his museum staff could not identify some of them. 'The makers did not put names on them, presumably because at that time it would have been obvious to all.'

The Worst Pub

In 1995 the Polar Bear in Soho was named the worst pub in London by the listings magazine *Time Out*. Business immediately shot up by 60 per cent. By the time they had erected a banner outside saying 'The Worst Pub in the West End', it was impossible to get in.

Describing the pub's unique ambience, the article highlighted not only its nine television screens that were always on and its ample supply of pinball machines, but also the fact that all the seats had come off in the ladies' lavatory. The general theme of the ravishing decor was described as 'jungle', which explains the inflatable monkeys, snakes and plastic foliage.

'This pub is disgusting,' said a thirty-year-old Irish bookie called Alan while stubbing out his cigarette on the carpet. 'The carpet is rank, the bar needs a wipe, the decoration is crap and it's very expensive. But it has a good atmosphere. It's full of morons who just want to get off their heads.'

Bass Taverns, the pub's owner, were very happy. 'We were planning a complete refurbishment, but now we'll have to think again,' a spokesman said.

The Least Successful Aftershave

The top male fragrance for people of our tastes is the exquisite Ieuan No. 14. In 1995 a go-ahead perfume company decided to launch a new line of aftershave. Boldly, they named it after Ieuan Evans, the Welsh rugby international winger. It was withdrawn after selling only thirty bottles because women did not want their menfolk smelling like a rugby player.

This is now the most exclusive fragrance in the world as only thirty people on the planet walk round smelling of it. It is extremely difficult to get hold of. 'I do have a few bottles of the stuff,' Mr Evans wrote in his memoirs, so you might have to get some from him.

The Least Successful Marketing Ploy

The supreme victor in the marketing field is the unbeatable Hoover offer of 1992. Hoping to shift a backlog of vacuum cleaners, they offered two free air tickets to anywhere in Europe to every customer who spent £100 on a Hoover product.

They were soon inundated when people realised that the prize was worth several times more than the purchase. In a moment of absolute genius Hoover now pulled out all the stops and extended the offer to American flights as well. There was even a TV campaign ending with the words: 'Two Return Seats: Unbelievable.'

In what was correctly described as 'the free offer to end all free offers' they provided tickets for 220,000 people and even started chartering their own planes to meet the demand. It cost £48 million to give pleasure to so many. This was life-enhancing generosity in an age of naked commercial self-interest.

The Least Successful Freelance Commission

Thoroughly impressed by Jeff Dodd's metalwork, an Egyptian businessman invited him to build fifty floats for a major trade fair in Alexandria in 1989. Accepting the offer immediately, Mr Dodd flew to Egypt.

The idea was to complete the job in a month, but it was ten days before any of the workforce arrived. When the forty workers did eventually turn up, they were all good people and very willing, but none of them had worked with metal before or spoke any English.

When it became obvious that fifty floats were out of the question, this was reduced to four, including one covered in flowers for EgyptAir. The flowers were later cancelled. When four floats also proved impossible, because the metal was arriving very slowly by horse and cart, the parade was postponed until the following year.

Helpfully, EgyptAir said they still wanted their float to celebrate the delivery of some new planes at a big publicity event in Cairo. This meant taking the float all the way from Alexandria. It was already fifty feet long and thirteen feet high and built on top of a Chevrolet truck, but all of it now had to go on a very tall lorry to be transported. According to Mr Dodd, the driver 'left a trail of tree branches and greenery and telephone lines' before scraping a footbridge and damaging the float.

When they arrived in Cairo the promised workshop in which to finish the float turned out to be a farmyard. The tent in which they were to work was not yet constructed. 'The float was damaged, there was no tent and there were little jumping fleas and mosquitoes all over the ground,' Mr Dodd recalled.

The idea had been to take the completed float on a ten-day, 621-mile parade from Cairo to Port Said, ending up at the International Egyptian Car Rally. Mr Dodd had worked continuously for thirty-six hours before the parade, when it was found that President Mubarak was doing a tour of the country and all public functions were curtailed. 'In the end there was no parade at all so they had to take back the truck, and as far as I know the floats are still in the tent.'

Returning to his native Spalding, Mr Dodd said he would not have missed the experience for anything.

The Worst Restaurant Name

Only when the German consul-general personally suggested 'something less controversial' did Punit Shablok, a Mumbai businessman, concede that it might have been a mistake to call his new restaurant Hitler's Cross. Admitting that he was not a student of western history, he was surprised to hear that the name refers to a medal given by the Führer to German mothers of large families.

On 18 August 2006, *le tout* Mumbai, including film stars and the mayor, arrived for the opening night to find by the front door a portrait of Hitler addressing the Nuremberg rally. Inside Mr Shablok had bought a number of swastika flags to hang on the walls alongside posters of Nazi propaganda. There were also Nazi symbols on the menu.

Baffled by the fuss, Mr Shablok said he wanted a name with an authentically European ring that would stand out in the crowded restaurant market. He was hoping to open two more branches in Mumbai before October.

The Least Successful Promotional Offer

In so many sports the players get all the exercise, while the spectators are more sedentary than is really good for their cardiovascular systems. The baseball game between Texas Rangers and the Cleveland

Indians, however, set a better example.

Wishing to attract a larger crowd to the game in June 1974, the Cleveland Indians offered as much beer as you could drink at only ten cents a glass. A total of 25,134 fans arrived at Cleveland Municipal Stadium instead of the usual eight thousand, many of them already inebriated. They were soon out of their seats.

In a carnival atmosphere, Rangers were leading 5–1 when a heavyset woman ran into the centre circle, bared her enormous, unhindered breasts to appreciative applause and then tried to kiss the umpire, Nestor Chylak, who was not in a kissing mood.

This fine woman soon inspired everyone else. A naked man now sprinted to second base and, as security guards chased after him, a father and son also ran out and mooned at the fans.

Interest in the game itself was peaking when Rangers' Mike Hargrove was pelted with hotdogs. Things came to a head in the ninth innings when a fan attempted to steal Texas outfielder Jeff Burroughs's cap. Confronting the fan, Mr Burroughs tripped. Thinking he had been attacked, Rangers' manager charged onto the field, followed by his players wielding bats.

At this point the live TV broadcast was suspended and the local radio began live riot coverage instead. When a large number of fans surged onto the field, some taking their stadium seats with them, there was a rain of beer from the stands. The Indians' manager, Ken Aspromonte, now ordered his players to grab bats and defend their opponents against the crowd.

Boxing broke out all over the pitch and the rain of beer gave way to a hail of cups, golf balls, popcorn containers, hotdogs, cheeseburgers, folding chairs and anything else that was not bolted down.

Sated with nudity and pugilism, the umpire forfeited the game to Texas and later called the fans 'uncontrollable beasts', stating that he had never seen anything like it 'except in the zoo'.

The riot squad were called to restore order as the players ran for their lives, getting some exercise at last.

The Worst Timetable

Always striving for something better, the *Great Britain Railway Passenger Timetable* of 1995 was a model of its kind. Thanks to privatisation, a company called Railtrack took over this publication. They got off to a rip-roaring start when the 2,100-page work contained so many errors that it required a fifty-seven-page supplement to correct them all.

For connoisseurs the first timetable was only ever a workmanlike performance and the supplement itself was a far greater work. Protean and fizzing with mistakes, its fifty-seven pages needed a second supplement of corrections that ran to 246 pages.

This was impressive enough, but real excitement started to mount when a Railtrack spokesman said the second supplement was bejewelled with errors also. This may not have had the sheer superabundance of earlier versions, but the errors in the second supplement were far superior to those in either the first supplement or the original volume.

Phil Wilkes, a spokesman for the railway passenger watchdog, said: 'Trains appear on one page, but disappear before they get to their destination.' An air of mystery is something really quite new in railway timetables.

To give you some idea of the value for money involved here, Mr Wilkes said that if they issued a third supplement 'you would need a holdall to carry it around'.

Barry Doe, a timetable expert, said: 'I have timetables going back to the 1950s and this is by far the worst I have seen.' The only real sadness is that all eighty thousand copies of this great work were pulped before posterity could treasure it.

The Least Successful Committee Meeting

The key event in the history of local government was the meeting of the recreation committee of Bude–Stratton Town Council in December 1987 which was convened and adjourned without a single item of business being discussed. 'Never in my thirty years on the council', said Councillor Paul Laxton, 'have I known anything like it.'

Resigning in protest, he wrote to the council chairman, pointing out that although the agenda was packed with matters relating to Bude leisure provision, these were put on hold when Councillor Dick Willoughby arrived with his pet terrier, Chamois.

Invited to leave him outside with another member's dog, Councillor Willoughby robustly declined. There ensued a boisterous discussion about Chamois's democratic rights. Councillor Laxton considered putting down a motion about dogs in the chamber, but said it was a complete waste of paper.

Speaking about this fine committee, with which any of us would wish to be associated, he said: 'I have come to the conclusion that it is unable to differentiate between doing things the right way and doing things the wrong way.'

☞ 4 ☜

LEADING BY EXAMPLE

The Business of Politics

A Party Leader for Us
The Least Successful Parliamentary Question
The Least Successful British Prime Minister
The Least Successful Election
The Least Successful Education Manifesto
The Worst Use of English as She Is Spoke
The Least Lively Candidates
The Least Successful Practical Joke

The Military Mind

The Worst Anti-Aircraft Weapon
The Least Successful Unsinkable Warship
The Most Chaotic Commemoration
The Least Successful Eternal Flame
The Worst Background Music

'Try as hard as we may for perfection, the net result of our labours is an amazing variety of imperfectness. We are surprised at our own versatility in being able to fail in so many ways.'

SAMUEL McCHORD CROTHERS,
MINISTER AND ESSAYIST

A Party Leader for Us

Lord Pearson of Rannoch became the most important politician ever when in August 2010 he stood down as leader of the UK Independence Party because it 'deserves someone better'.

Politicians are not noted for admitting error or their own shortcomings so Lord Pearson made history with one radical sentence: 'I have learned that I'm not much good at party politics.'

A donnish fellow, he had brought a breath of fresh air to the general election campaign, particularly when attempting to recall parts of the UKIP manifesto during a TV interview with Jon Sopel the previous April. The great man could not, for example, cast light on UKIP's policy of getting retired police officers to act as wardens on housing estates, patrolling car parks, lift shafts and so on:

'Have you asked retired police if they want to do this?'
'I imagine we've had a few conversations.'
'Do you know if you have?'
'I haven't personally had any conversations with retired police officers. I have to say I haven't . . .'
'Have you read your manifesto?'

[73]

'Of course.'

'Really?'

'Yup.'

'You don't seem very familiar with it.'

'I haven't remembered it all in detail. I didn't come on to talk about this sort of thing.'

'You didn't come on to talk about your manifesto?'

'I did, but not in the detail of whether I've talked to some policeman in some car park.

After his resignation Lord Pearson said: 'I need to give more time to my wider interests.' Well, absolutely.

The Least Successful Parliamentary Question

It is a rule of question time in the New Zealand parliament that MPs must read their questions to the house exactly as they are written on the order paper, which is a grotesque infringement of the right to free speech. Lesser politicians, dull of mind and spirit, usually manage this within the permitted three attempts, but Alec Neale MP showed just what can be done even with a simple question about rabbit damage in the South Island.

On the order paper in February 1991 his question to the minister asked: 'Has he received any reports on the ecological and environmental problems attributable to rabbits in the Central South Island; if so, what do they say?'

He started off quietly enough, inserting the word 'disaster' after 'ecological', but he had not really warmed up and was told to try again. Then from nowhere came a flash of utter brilliance. He read out every word correctly, but in the wrong order, which brought gasps of admiration from the house. Could he pull off the treble? Yes he could. In a moment of deft subtlety the word 'attributable' came out as 'attributed' and the house erupted.

The speaker rose for a third and final time to suggest moving on to another question. Thankfully, the opposition leader, Michael Moore, sensing that the great man was on a roll and yet to reach his peak, said that Mr Neale should not be stopped now.

Offered one last chance, he did not disappoint, saving his greatest artistry for the end. Rising to his feet, he decided to make absolutely sure and in a witty final flourish he read out the punctuation as well. When he came to the semi-colon he read out 'full stop' and the house exploded in a storm of appreciative comments as the question was abandoned.

In the closing tributes the former prime minister David Lange said that six million rabbits had been born in the time that this great parliamentarian was on his feet.

The Least Successful British Prime Minister

William Pulteney, the first Earl of Bath, stands triumphantly at the top of any list of British prime ministers: he held the highest office in the land for two days. It is known to historians as 'the Short-Lived Ministry', which has a certain ring to it.

Invited to form a government on 10 February 1746, he was unable to find more than one person who would agree to serve in his cabinet. He abandoned the attempt after forty-eight hours, fifty-two minutes and eleven seconds.

Acknowledging the complete success of his period in office, a satirist at the time wrote that he 'never transacted one rash thing and, what is more marvellous, left as much money in the Treasury as he found in it'.

The Least Successful Election

In the definitive council election of 1994 for the Bartons ward of West Oxfordshire, nobody voted at all, nobody stood for election and there was no polling booth.

Everywhere else in the country politicians were making promises they could not keep and party activists were disturbing people in their homes with pushy leaflets, but the Bartons had no such inconvenience. There were no arguments, no personality clashes and no policy disagreements.

Apart from the positioning of the Middle Barton noticeboard, nobody could identify any key local issues.

'You can see why people aren't clawing each other's eyes out to stand as candidates,' explained Eric Bennett, a Liberal Democrat activist from nearby Chipping Norton.

The Least Successful Education Manifesto

In April 1994 Conservatives on Derby City Council produced an education manifesto entitled *It's All About Standards.* Now a collector's item, it was found to contain nineteen spelling, grammar and punctuation errors in its three pages. 'I hold my hand up,' said Councillor Martin du Sautoy, basking in the glory.

The Worst Use of English as She Is Spoke

Blessed with a gift for mangling the English language, Joseph 'Erap' Estrada, the vice-president of the Philippines, had a wrong word for every occasion. Interviewed once on television, he was asked if he had been asthmatic when young. 'That's not true,' he replied angrily. 'I've always been a Catholic.'

He regularly thanked audiences for giving him 'a standing ovulation' and was once so piqued by people criticising his English that he threatened to speak only in the local language of Tagalog. 'From now on I'll just speak in the binocular,' he said.

Praised for remembering people's names, he explained that he had 'a pornographic memory'. Asked why he regularly patronised the same restaurant, he replied: 'I like the ambulance.'

In 1994 a former schoolmate published a satirical book with cartoons entitled *ERAPtion: How to Speak English without Really Trial,* bringing together all the great man's most distinguished utterances. It is the only known work of satire that made its victim so popular he ordered it to be distributed with his presidential campaign manifesto.

The Least Lively Candidates

In June 2008 the Romanian village of Voinesti re-elected their deceased mayor, Neculai Ivascu, by thirty-seven votes, preferring him to the living candidate. 'It's not the time for change,' a voter told Romanian television. This was not the first or last occasion it had happened.

In November 2000 Mel Carnahan became the first ever person to get elected to the American Senate having already passed away. He won the seat for Missouri after a campaign in which his supporters had employed the slogan 'I'm still with Mel'.

In 2009 Missouri was at it again when the town of

Winfield re-elected their mayor, Harry Stonebraker, four months after his demise. It was the first time anyone had been comprehensively thrashed by a deceased candidate. Stonebraker got 90 per cent of the vote, easily trouncing Alderman Bernie Panther. 'His death only seemed to bolster his popularity,' said the *New York Daily News*.

By October 2009 the whole thing had taken off and the voters of Washington County in Pennsylvania were spoiled for choice in the general election with three deceased candidates on the ballot sheet. In 2010 it was entirely normal when Tracy City, Tennessee, elected the late Carl Geary. His widow, Susan, said his election 'was not a surprise at all to me. The day he passed away people were calling to say "We will still be voting for him."'

By November 2010 it was par for the course when Jenny Oropeza was re-elected to the California state senate post-mortem, easily beating her Republican rival.

On a racial equality note it is important to record that in 1964 Patsy Takemoto Mink was a trailblazing politician who became the first woman of colour to be elected to the American House of Representatives. In November 2002 she became the first deceased woman of colour to be elected to the American House of Representatives, a few weeks after her state funeral.

There is developing here what commentators call a trend.

The Least Successful Practical Joke

In the 1994 Danish general election Jacob Haugaard stood for parliament as a practical joke. His manifesto included free beer, nicer Christmas gifts, more Renaissance furniture in IKEA, Nutella in all army field rations, continuously green traffic lights, the introduction of several whales into Randers Fjord, the right to impotency, a tail wind on all cycle paths and the reclassification of people without a sense of humour as disabled. To support his candidacy he wrote a book entitled *If Work Is Healthy Give It to the Sick.*

The joke backfired, however, when this fine man not only got elected with a staggering 23,253 votes, but also had one of his manifesto policies made law: Nutella in all army field rations.

After an official first visit to Queen Margarethe at the Amalienborg Palace in Copenhagen, the stunned new MP for Aarhus said: 'It was all a practical joke, honestly. I guess people elected me because my promises are just as trustworthy as those of conventional political parties.'

Mr Haugaard had earlier played with a spoof punk band whose most notable song was entitled 'My House Has No Toilet'. He decided not to stand for re-election. He is the only non-minister to have his portrait hanging in the Danish parliament.

THE MILITARY MIND

The Worst Anti-Aircraft Weapon

The US Army's new M247 DIVAD mobile anti-air-craft gun showed enormous potential in early tests when its radar proved unable to distinguish between trees and helicopters. It was specially equipped with a fabulous twenty-ton gun turret that was too slow to track fast-moving targets, had serious problems operating in the cold weather and sprang numer-ous hydraulic leaks.

So far so good, but things got even better in Feb-ruary 1982 when the computer-controlled proto-type was demonstrated to military top brass and members of Congress. Once activated, it immedi-ately aimed its gun at the VIP review stand, caus-ing several minor injuries as members of the group jumped for cover. Throughout the demonstration it never successfully hit a sample target, but it did blow a three-hundred-metre crater in the ground.

A spokesman for the manufacturer claimed that these problems were due to the vehicle being washed for the demonstration. He had no explan-ation for why it had mistaken a latrine fan for a moving target and blown it to pieces.

Understandably keen to get this key weapon into production as soon as possible, Secretary of State for Defense Caspar Weinberger ordered a $54 million series of battlefield-condition tests in 1984. These were very special even by the DIVAD's high standards.

Unable to hit drones moving in a straight line, the DIVAD was given extra help. Even when they hovered motionless above it, the radar was unable to lock onto the target. The testers started adding radar reflectors to the drones to make them easier to spot. The *Atlantic Monthly* magazine said it was like 'demonstrating the abilities of a bloodhound by having it find a man standing alone in the middle of an empty parking lot, covered with steaks'.

The project was cancelled in 1985 and most of the prototypes ended up as extremely effective targets on air-force bombing ranges.

The Least Successful Unsinkable Warship

Hailed as the world's first unsinkable warship in 1863, the USS *Keokuk* was part of the Monitor class and shaped like a submarine. The thinking was that incoming shells would bounce off its curved sides. 'If they can have her ready in 120 days she will clean out every defensive unit in the South,' wrote Captain Alexander C. Rhind, her commander in the American Civil War.

During its first and last action it fired only three rounds while getting in return ninety direct hits, of which nineteen were on or below the waterline.

'Riddled like a colander', according to a signal from Captain Rhind, it sank in shallow water with only its shot-spattered funnel showing above the waves.

The Most Chaotic Commemoration

On 6 January 1994, peace reigned in Europe until plans were announced to mark the fiftieth anniversary of D-Day.

After only forty-eight hours Dame Vera Lynn, the forces' sweetheart, said she was very upset because she had not been invited. The Ministry of Defence in Paris issued a map of Normandy with a programme of events that put all the wartime beaches and battlefields in the wrong places. Next, plans to hold a ceremony at the celebrated Pegasus Bridge faltered when it was discovered that the French had pulled it down in a fit of modernisation.

The event took a completely unexpected turn when Britain's only woman Spitfire pilot, Carolyn Grace, convinced the RAF that she should be allowed to fly over the D-Day ceremony in a very old Spitfire with its original pilot, Flying Officer Johnny Houlton, sitting in the back seat. According to Mrs Grace, this would make a fitting tribute to her late husband, Nick, who had refurbished the plane in his spare time.

The RAF put it to the French, but they were not impressed by the prospect of a fly-past by a forty-two-year-old Australian housewife from Essex and her elderly passenger. Besides, all air traffic between Paris and Normandy was banned on the day for security reasons.

French farmers then revealed plans for a tractor blockade of the N13 from Cherbourg to Caen, which is the main road to the invasion beaches, in protest against big dairies knocking four centimes off the price they would pay for milk. Then British troops made a commemorative parachute jump into Normandy and were sent a £5,000 bill for crop damage.

Meanwhile in Britain, Dame Vera and all the veterans were now threatening to boycott the government's entire centrepiece celebrations because they were frivolous and involved spam fritter competitions.

Connoisseurs of mayhem looked on with growing admiration and Brigadier Tom Longland said that organising the commemoration had been 'more complicated than D-Day'.

The Least Successful Eternal Flame

The eternal flame at the cemetery in Kaliningrad, Russia, was lit in honour of fallen soldiers amidst pomp and ceremony at the end of the Second World War in 1945. It was turned off in April 1993 to save gas.

The Worst Background Music

The Royal Canadian Legion, an organisation for old soldiers from the Second World War, was extremely pleased with the radio commercial for its 2005 lottery. It was pulled from the airwaves on the first day of transmission, however, when it emerged that the background music they had selected was the Nazi Party anthem.

Entitled the 'Horst Wessel Lied', it features the booming drums and energetic brass typical of marching songs. It expresses the hope that 'the street will be free for stormtroopers' and contains the line 'Millions, full of hope, look up at the swastika'. A regulation in the 1934 sheet music makes it clear that the right arm has to be raised in the Hitler salute whenever the first and fourth verses are sung.

'It sounds good,' said Harvey Shevalier, a veteran of peacekeeping missions and first vice-president of the Alberta and Northwest Territories command for the Legion. 'But it was not the appropriate kind of music. That's why it was taken off. It should never have happened.'

The music had been judged suitable by the Legion's lottery committee. Laurel Harris, a media director for their marketing company, said the song was selected from a random tape of marching music that did not have titles on it.

5

THE INTELLECTUAL CONTRIBUTION

The Least Successful Philosophical Argument
The Least Successful Lecture
The Least Poetic Subject I
The Least Poetic Subject II
The Least Impressed Critic
The Least Successful Theatrical Experiment
The Least Successful Conference
The Most Incomprehensible Sentence
The Worst Photography Exhibition
The Least Successful Mensa Outing
The Most Implausible Book Title
The Least Successful Scientific Research Finding
The Worst Choice of Keynote Speaker
The Worst Description of Sex in a Novel

'All of us have failed to match our dreams of perfection. So I rate us on the basis of our splendid failure to do the impossible.'

WILLIAM FAULKNER

The Least Successful Philosophical Argument

Acclaimed as 'France's greatest living philosopher', Bernard-Henri Lévy pushed freedom of thought to new limits in 2010 when he published a magnificent book attacking Immanuel Kant as 'a fake'. Clinching his argument beyond any reasonable doubt, he cited the little-known thinker Jean-Baptiste Botul's immortal volume *The Sex Life of Immanuel Kant*, which reaches exactly the same conclusion.

He was halfway through his triumphant book tour, singing the praises of Botulism and its central theory ('the metaphysics of the flabby'), when some know-all pointed out that Botul was invented by a journalist in 1999 as part of a smarty-pants hoax. He even has a Wikipedia entry describing him as 'a fictional philosopher'.

The extent to which Botul (or any of us) actually exists is a large philosophical question and Professor Lévy swatted aside these complaints with bold, free-thinking indifference. 'It's the role of the philosopher to land blows,' he said, reasonably enough.

The Least Successful Lecture

As part of Richmond's seventeenth annual literature festival in November 2008, Professor A. C. Grayling, of Birkbeck College, London, was due to give a lecture on duty. He forgot to attend.

The Least Poetic Subject I

Solyman Brown was the first dentist-poet in the English language. His epic work in five cantos, *The Dentologia – a Poem on the Diseases of the Teeth* (1833), is one of the few poems in any language with a useful appendix listing three hundred qualified dental practitioners in America.

His poem could have been told in prose in a third of the time, but Mr Brown made the effort. This work is also much enlivened by footnotes giving sensible advice on dental hygiene, which were especially compiled for him by his great friend 'Eleazar Parmly, dentist'.

Among the blood-curdling examples of oral neglect contained in the fifth canto he relates the dental traumas of Serafina, who used to sing in the village choir, but had to give it up due to tooth rot. We are asked to imagine that 'the heavenly music of her lip / So sweet, the labouring bees might stop to sip' was replaced by a series of unmelodic whistling sounds and quite possibly a lisp:

> Ye ask the cause: – by premature decay,
> Two of her dental pearls have passed away;
> The two essential to those perfect strains,
> That charm the soul when heavenly music
>   reigns.

But hope is not lost and this is where the three hundred dental practitioners come in:

> . . . The dental art
> Can every varying tone with ease restore
> And give the music sweeter than before.

In his masterly work *The Joy of Bad Verse*, Nicholas T. Parsons wisely suggests that this poem may benefit from recitation.

The Least Poetic Subject II

All too few poets have grappled with the heady subject of science, but Margaret Cavendish, Duchess of Newcastle, got stuck in. She was always willing to have a stab at a whole range of unlikely questions in the face of which others have baulked.

In 'The Reason Why Thoughts Are Only in the Head' (1653), for example, she sorts out why we do not think in any other part of our anatomy; our heels, for example, which do seem in most respects perfectly well suited to the activity.

> For had the heels such quantity of brain,
> Which doth the head, and skull therein contain,

> Then would such thoughts, which in the brain dwell
> high,
> Descend down low, and in the heel would lie.

Showing no signs of tiredness, she continues:

> As in the skull then might the toe or knee
> Had they an optic nerve, both hear and see,
> And sinews room, fancy therein to breed
> Copies of verses might from the heel proceed.

Among other things she explains why water quenches fire, why the sea makes a roaring sound, why getting burned stings, what causes an echo (she is not absolutely conclusive on this one) and how to tell if something is a liquid:

> That is liquid which is moist and wet
> Fire that property can never get.

On neurology she is especially sound. 'The fairies in the brain may be the cause of many thoughts.' Even after all these years this is still the best explanation and probably correct. Her reflections upon the cause of saltiness in sea water, however, involved asking the opinion of fish, which proved problematic.

> Who knows, but fishes which swim in the Sea
> Can give a reason why so Salt it be?

Her 1653 poem 'Air' addresses the challenging question of why, no matter where you look, you will find a ready supply of the stuff. Look to the right and there it is. Look to the left. There it is again.

Up, down, wherever, air is everywhere. Why so? It is a good question. She put it down to long atoms.

In a more personal vein she once wrote verses about a friend who had urged her to stop writing poetry:

> Then pity take, do the world a good turn
> And all you write, cast in the fire and burn.

This outrageous suggestion only drove her on. Her range extended beyond science and she also wrote a biography of her husband, the Duke, in which he was compared favourably with Julius Caesar.

An attempt to translate her poetry into Latin was abandoned when the language proved un-equal to it.

The Least Impressed Critic

The writer Graham Greene was at his most savage when reviewing a new film called *21 Days*, which had been adapted from a short play by John Galsworthy. Writing in the *Spectator* of 1940, he observed: 'I have no good word to say of it. The brilliant acting of Mr Hay Petrie as a decayed and outcast curate cannot conquer the overpowering flavour of cooked ham.'

Awash in unforgiving vitriol, he complained that 'for the rather dubious merits of the original the adapter has substituted incredible coincidences and banal situations', adding that he found the

whole film 'slow, wordy and unbearably sentimen-
tal'. Only at the end of the article did Mr Greene
announce that he had, in fact, written the screen-
play himself.

The Least Successful Theatrical Experiment

Theatrical experimentation reached new and breath-
taking heights at Frankfurt's prestigious Schauspiel-
haus theatre in August 2010 during a production
of *Moscow Towards the End of the Line*, which the programme notes described as 'a crazy depiction of
one of the most famous alcoholic benders in Russian literature'.

Appearing in this adaptation of Victor Erofeyev's
satirical novel about binge-drinking Soviet workers
on a railway journey, four of Germany's top actors
decided 'as an experiment' to substitute vodka for
water in all stage props. 'At first it was quite impressive. They seemed to be giving a good imperson-
ation of tipsiness,' one audience member told a
German newspaper. 'Then they started leaping
around shouting "Cheers" in Russian and then they
handed round the drink.'

One of the actors could no longer stand up.
Another started reading from his script. He later
put it on the floor and forgot where it was until
another actor slipped on it and fell. 'People
started clapping thinking it belonged to the per-

formance,' the theatregoer said.

In many ways this production improved upon Erofeyev's original. The ending was much more dramatic: suddenly one of the actors fell off the stage and another fell from a table on which he was unexpectedly standing. The reality–art barrier was then excitingly shattered when the backstage crew intervened and called an ambulance. Making himself heard above the siren, the star of the show roared and raged like King Lear upon the heath, except that medics called for police backup. He later had his stomach pumped at Frankfurt's university clinic.

The Least Successful Conference

In March 2001, the Public Health Laboratory Service held a food-poisoning conference in Colindale to discuss water-borne infection. Naturally, thirty of the seventy-eight delegates went down with food poisoning. 'They were poisoned by their lunch,' a spokesman said. 'It might have been a water-borne infection.' Theory is all well and good, but nothing can ever replace first-hand experience.

The Most Incomprehensible Sentence

Between 1995 and 1998 Denis Dutton organised the Bad Writing Contest. Each year it sought to find the most incomprehensible sentence published in academic books or journals, as judged by Mr Dutton himself and his editorial staff on the scholarly journal *Philosophy and Literature.*

Some sentences are too important to understand and it would be difficult to improve upon the 1996 winner from *Plato Etc: The Problems of Philosophy and Their Resolution* by Professor Roy Bhaskar. In an age of soundbites, when everything is being dumbed down, we should be extremely grateful to Professor Bhaskar for remaining on the intellectual high ground:

Indeed dialectical critical realism may be seen under the aspect of Foucauldian strategic reversal – of the unholy trinity of Parmenidean/Platonic/Aristotelian provenance; of the Cartesian–Lockean–Humean–Kantian paradigm, of foundationalisms (in practice, fideistic foundationalisms) and irrationalisms (in practice, capricious exercises of the will-to-power or some other ideologically and/or psycho-somatically buried source) new and old alike: of the primordial failing of western philosophy, ontological monovalence, and its close ally, the epistemic fallacy with its ontic dual; of the analytic problematic laid down by Plato, which Hegel served only to replicate in his actualist monovalent analytic reinstatement in transfigurative reconciling dialectical connection, while in his hubristic claims for absolute idealism he inaugurated the Comtean, Kierkegaardian and Nietzschean eclipses of reason, replicating the fundaments of positivism through its transmutation route to the superidealism of a Baudrillard.

[96]

'It's a splendid piece of prose and I'm certain many of us will now attempt to read it aloud without taking a breath,' said Mr Dutton. 'The jacket blurb, incidentally, informs us that this is the author's most accessible book to date.'

The Worst Photography Exhibition

The Impressions Gallery in York captured the public imagination in April 1994 when it held an acclaimed exhibition based upon a public appeal for bad photographs. In no time it was inundated with top-class work. This included a photograph of a prized new car with only the number plate in focus, a Christmas Day snap by Bethany Hill, then aged three, which just shows her grandfather's feet in slippers, and a black-as-night shot supposedly showing David Bowie live at Milton Keynes.

'All the pictures have created great interest and are works of art in their own right. I've been media blitzed. Thousands of people are turning up to see them,' said the gallery director, Paul Wombell.

Particularly acclaimed was the work of Tom Pemberton. On a trip to Whitby he put his wife's Instamatic camera to his eye the wrong way round. The resulting shot was a sensitive and thrillingly blurred view of his left ear with a thin sliver of Whitby in crystal-clear focus behind it. Generating understandable media attention, Mr Pemberton's ear provoked press interviews as far away as Johannesburg and Canada.

The Least Successful Mensa Outing

Described in the local paper as 'twenty-five of the brainiest people in the world', a delegation of Mensa members visited the Science Museum in Bristol when it opened in March 1991. The group was led in person by Victor Serebriakoff, the international president of Mensa, an organisation for people of unusually high IQ.

The museum was right next door to the railway station, a short seventy-five-yard walk down the railway parade. Not one of them could find it.

'When they didn't arrive we got quite worried. You can't miss it,' said the museum manager, who sent out a search party. 'We finally found them wandering around a side street like a bunch of lost sheep.'

The Most Implausible Book Title

Now in its thirty-second triumphant year, the *Bookseller*/Diagram Prize is awarded annually to the book with the oddest title of the year. It got off to a strong start in 1978 with *Proceedings of the Second International Workshop on Nude Mice* and stormed on to *Theory of Lengthwise Rolling* in 1983.

Other high spots included *Greek Rural Postmen and Their Cancellation Numbers* and *Weeds in a Changing World*. In 2004 *Bombproof Your Horse* sounded slightly too interesting for some tastes, but the competition got back on course with *The Stray Shopping Carts of Eastern North America: A Guide to Field Identification* and *Crocheting Adventures with Hyperbolic Planes*.

The 2008 winner, entitled *The 2009–2014 World Outlook for 60-Milligram Containers of Fromage Frais*, proved controversial because it was written not by its listed author, Philip M. Parker, but by a machine of Mr Parker's invention.

The prize was not awarded in 1987 and 1991 because the entries were not thought to be odd enough.

The Least Successful Scientific Research Finding

After an extensive research programme testing the slipperiness of banana skins in different states of decay, Chris McDonnell concluded that the fruit was not hazardous and the idea of people skidding on them was a myth 'confined to comic books and cartoons'.

It is hardly necessary to announce that in April 2004, while rushing towards a store entrance during a shopping expedition in his native Canterbury,

Mr McDonnell revised his research findings in view of new evidence when he skidded on a banana skin, lost his footing, fell over and sat down sharply on the pavement. 'My initial opinion', he said, 'was upended.'

The Worst Choice of Keynote Speaker

In January 1996 the British Council organised a seminar entitled 'How Can Democracy Be Sustained?' The keynote speaker, Brigadier Julius Maada Bio of Sierra Leone, was unable to attend, however, as he had just overthrown his country's government in an army coup and his first decree was to cancel the forthcoming elections.

The Worst Description of Sex in a Novel

Founded in 1993 to acclaim the year's worst writing about sex, the annual Bad Sex Award has maintained a consistently high standard. The novelist Ian McEwan is on record as saying that it is the most coveted prize in English literature.

In 2000 Sean Thomas was understandably ebullient as he beat off a challenge from John Updike with a coital moment involving a particularly squat girlfriend.

It is time, time . . . Now. Yes. She is so small and compact and yet she has all the necessary features . . . Shall

I compare thee to a Sony Walkman, thou art more compact and more – she is his own Toshiba, his dinky little JVC, his sweet Aiwa . . . Aiwa, aiwa, aiwa aiwa aiwa aiwa aiwa aiwa aiwa aiwaaaaaaaaahhhhhhhhh.

'It's an enormous honour and I'm gratified,' Mr Thomas said. 'I knew I had a very good chance of winning it.'

In 2004 Tom Wolfe won golden opinions with a sentence from *I Am Charlotte Simmons*: 'Slither slither slither slither went the tongue, but the hand, that was what she tried to concentrate on, the hand, since it has the entire terrain of her torso to explore and not just the otorhinolaryngological caverns . . .'

Iain Hollingshead won in 2006 when his first novel wowed the judges with his classic description of some 'bulging trousers'. Obviously delighted to become the prize's youngest ever winner, he said: 'I hope to win it every year.'

Although intended for novels, the prize received a rare nomination in 2010 for a work of non-fiction, the memoirs of Tony Blair. 'I needed that love Cherie gave me, selfishly,' he wrote. The racy paragraph, which had readers all over the globe spitting out their cornflakes, continued: 'I devoured it to give me strength, I was an animal following my instinct, knowing I would need every ounce of emotional power and resilience to cope with what lay ahead.' It was a fine passage in which Mr Blair showed that he was so much more than just a prime minister.

6

DOING IT WHEN YOU'RE OUT AND ABOUT

Off Duty

The Worst Guidebook
The Least Successful After-Dinner Speech
Our Sort of Bomb
The Worst Conker Players
The Least Successful Parking
The Most Boring Hobby
Streaking: How to Do It
The Worst Flower Show
The Most Boring Postcard
The Most Chaotic Attempt to Break a
World Record
The Least Successful Attempt to Go to the Toilet
The Most Confused Suicide Attempt
The Worst Luxury Day Trip
The Worst Days Out
The Most Accident-Prone Person (Scotland)
The Worst Twelfth Night

Motoring News

The Least Successful Lucky Charm
The Murray Walker Lifetime Achievement Award
The Most Speeding Offences in One Go
The Worst Car
The Worst Car Thief in Russia

All at Sea

The World Cruise that Went Nowhere
The Least Successful Sea Rescue
The Least Successful Ice Patrol

*

'The happy people are failures because they are
on such good terms with themselves they don't
give a damn.'
AGATHA CHRISTIE

The Worst Guidebook

In a quantum leap for this genre, the 1988/9 official guidebook for tourists in Boston failed to correctly locate every major landmark in the area. This essential volume said that the Amtrak station on Dartmouth Street was in Newbury Street and that the shopping area, which actually is in Newbury Street, was on Storrow Drive.

It placed both the Four Seasons Hotel and the Ritz Carlton three streets away, and anyone trying to find the John B. Hynes Veterans' Memorial Convention Center would have been taken on an eye-opening adventure to distant Huntington Avenue.

This fine book, which could only encourage visitors to explore the city in greater detail, was published and sold by the tourist bureau. Its head office was also shown on the map as being several blocks from its actual location.

Understandably, the bureau gave the man in charge a large pay rise. 'He's underpaid,' said Thomas Kershaw, chairman of the bureau's board. 'We don't want to lose him.'

Later versions of the guidebook have failed to match it and have been crippled by accuracy.

The Least Successful After-Dinner Speech

Few after-dinner speakers have given more entertainment than the actor Ken McCoy, who in May 1994 dressed up as his ever-popular character Albert Crapper, the drunken tramp, to amuse members of the upmarket Alwoodley Golf Club in Yorkshire.

Kitted out in his moth-eaten flat cap, scarf and overcoat tied with string, he arrived at this lavish occasion, unshaven and made up with the purple nose and bright red cheeks of the serious drinker. Entering the luxurious four-star Forte Crest Hotel, he was immediately thrown out by a waiter.

Determined to give his speech, he next climbed in through a toilet window, but banged his head and emerged into the hotel foyer once more, now covered in blood. He was thrown out again, but this time by a burly golfer who threatened to call the police.

Making one final attempt, he dashed into the dining room, pursued by various golfers. He ran towards the top table full of bigwigs to explain who he was, but was rugby-tackled to the ground where everyone sat on him.

'It's just too dangerous,' said Mr McCoy, who decided to retire this character, explaining that the same thing had happened the week before at a rugby club event where the first team stripped off and squashed him.

Our Sort of Bomb

Digging near his home at Cottishall in Norfolk in September 2004, David Page unearthed a rusting piece of metal resembling a camping-gas cylinder. Only when he pushed the button at one end did it occur to him that this might be a highly dangerous unexploded bomb. Clearly something had to be done.

Sweating with fear, he phoned the police and was told not to let go. With tremendous ingenuity he taped the device to his hand so that he could not release the trigger-like button. 'I was absolutely terrified that I would be blown into a million pieces. The woman police operator kept saying it would be OK, but I said to her, "You're not the one holding the bomb."'

As an extra precaution he buried his hand in a barrel of sand. 'I thought, "If it does go off I'll hopefully only lose my arm."' What a man.

Police arrived and cordoned off a two-mile area, then called in the army. 'Tell my family I love them if the worst happens,' Mr Page told the police telephone operator. There was no need because his equally courageous wife Joanne now arrived and refused to leave his side.

As it turned out, the bomb was a Citroën car part. Was his courage in any way diminished by the facts? Of course not. Incredibly, there is no medal the Queen can give this brave man. Perhaps Citroën could honour him?

The Worst Conker Players

In October 1994 Martin Ashton and Mark Tuckey set a new all-comers' world record when they failed to hit each other's conker in one hundred attempts at an Isle of Wight regional championship final. It was a personal best.

Sadly, the referee stopped this enjoyable contest just as it was gathering momentum, so we shall never know what this in-form duo might have gone on to achieve. 'We thought we were doing quite well,' Mr Ashton said afterwards.

The Least Successful Parking

Before a Christmas shopping expedition, Mary Geeson made the most of her car's security lock while parking in Chesterfield. Having fitted one end around the brake pedal and the other to her steering wheel, she then turned her engine back on, wishing to drive forward into another space in front of her.

We have all done this in our time, but how many of us, like Mrs Geeson, can say that we then shot over the road, mounted the opposite pavement, smashed through a fence, hit a parked car, knocked the gears into reverse, sped backwards in a straight line and sent flying a would-be rescuer while we rammed backwards into a van which had now taken the parking space anyway?

The Most Boring Hobby

Fighting off stiff competition from one man who collects different varieties of traffic cone and another who spends his free time photographing brick walls, a gentleman answering only to the name of Gordon won 'The Most Boring Man of the Year' award in 1994. Interviewed on the *Vanessa* show, he said that he collected brown paper.

Describing one of his samples, our specialist said: 'This is one of my favourites. You can't find it everywhere, but if you're lucky you might spot it on a package or something you got sent through the post.' Gordon also collects *Mr Men* books.

Streaking: How to Do It

The plan was eminently sensible. On 14 January 2004 a trio of streakers would strip off in their car and leave the engine running outside for a quick getaway while they sprinted through Denny's twenty-four-hour restaurant in Spokane, Washington, wearing only shoes and hats despite the freezing weather. Nothing could be simpler. It was all very predictable until they glanced out of the window to see their 1988 Mazda, containing their clothes, being driven off by a car thief who had just finished his breakfast.

In a defining moment the streakers gave chase immediately, but the car had gone. They were hiding in the car park, discussing how they might best report this theft to the police, when they were themselves arrested.

The Worst Flower Show

The only horticultural event that interests us in the slightest is the Beadnell Alternative Flower Show, which flourished in Northumbria between 1987 and 1992. Founded by the pioneering Jennifer Hall to reflect the reality of local gardening, it was dedicated to lavishing prizes upon the worst flowers and produce in the region.

No potted perfection for them, no feuds and rivalry over the biggest bean, no nobbling of the best turnip, no round-the-clock guard to thwart leek-slashing skulduggery. At Beadnell there was only a sunlit upland of day-long goodwill. It attracted 150 entries a year and Mrs Hall was inundated with letters from people abroad wishing to set up a similar competition.

'The hardest task was finding an unqualified judge,' she explained.

Standards were high. The Best Weed cup was won by a plant that was fifteen feet tall. Every year new categories were added for horticulture and craft: the Most Unusual Jam, the Least Tempting Home-Made Sweets, and 'Hanging's Too Good for It' for the worst hanging-basket display.

In 1991 they added the 'What on Earth's That?' category for really advanced gardeners and the 'Unfinished Craft Item You Wish You Had Never Started'. In that same year they had a sponsor for the first time, but forgot to put his name in the programme.

The Most Boring Postcard

Worldwide interest was immediately sparked in 1992 when the Wiend Centre in Wigan announced that it would not only be holding an exhibition of the world's most boring postcards, but also unveiling the greatest work ever produced in this genre. Swamped with superlative exhibits from as far afield as Brazil, Mongolia and Tibet, the organisers said that early front-runners included a dimly lit view of a transport pontoon in Ulan Bator and 'Gasworks, Leeds, viewed from Adington Street toilets'.

'We think there's something for everyone,' said Brian Corrigan, the marketing officer of Wigan

Council. The winning entry was a postcard showing 'a staggeringly boring traffic interchange in Redditch'. It was sent in by Liz McParlin of Aberystwyth, who won 'a luxury weekend in Wigan'. Gil Swift crowned his career as Director of Leisure Services by opening this exhibition and then retired at the top.

The Most Chaotic Attempt to Break a World Record

Attempting to get into *The Guinness Book of Records* by playing his horn non-stop for thirty-two hours, Liam Kite arrived at a specially erected marquee at Tower Gardens, Skegness in August 1990. 'It has taken weeks to organise this,' said his mother, Marion Kite, whose son was eight and a half hours into his record-breaking attempt when a neighbour complained about the noise.

A policewoman arrived and told Mr Kite to stop playing immediately, but his mother mistook her for a strip-o-gram and told her son to keep going. 'Then she became very officious and threatened to arrest both me and Liam. I could not believe what was happening,' said Mrs Kite.

Her son accepted the offer of accommodation at a public lavatory belonging to the owner of the nearby amusement arcade. Still playing, he trooped over to the toilets with two official adjudicators, a timekeeper and the man in charge of his three horns. They then took up their positions in different cubicles as Mr Kite played on.

An hour later they were on the move again, this time to the foyer of a nearby cinema where arrangements had been made earlier for him to play through the night. There he developed a swollen lip and had to admit defeat, seventeen and a half hours into the attempt.

The Least Successful Attempt to Go to the Toilet

Desperate to relieve himself shortly after take-off on a flight to Hanover in January 1993, Johann Peter Grzeganek, a German tourist, could wait no longer despite the insistence of the cabin crew that he stay seated while the seatbelt sign was on.

It was far too late for this so Mr Grzeganek jumped up from his seat and, giving a top-drawer performance, shouted in German: 'I have to go urgently to the lavatory; otherwise I will go through the roof. I am exploding.'

Hearing the words '*Ich explodiere*', the cabin crew, who spoke no German, assumed he was a suicide bomber and alerted the pilot, who dumped all his fuel, turned round and made an emergency landing back at Fort Lauderdale airport, where Mr Grzeganek was arrested and imprisoned for ten months to await trial.

When his case eventually came to court the judge

dismissed it as ridiculous and apologised to him, but even then Mr Grzeganek went the extra mile. Rearrested outside the courtroom because his tourist visa had run out, he was sent back to prison in Miami to await deportation. In the hands of a real artist even the simplest everyday event can be transformed into a surreal drama of many acts.

The Most Confused Suicide Attempt

Deciding in 2008 that life was not worth living, a Porthcawl resident took his brother's car, rigged up a gas canister and drove to a beauty spot near Merthyr Tydfil. In that fateful hour he wound up the window and turned on the canister. Looking out across the beauty spot, he decided that life was worth living after all. To celebrate his change of heart he lit a cigarette, blew up the car and was taken to hospital where he was treated for burns.

Pleading guilty to unintentional arson, this good man, whom we cannot afford to lose, was given a twelve-month community order and told to complete a course of 'enhanced thinking skills'.

The Worst Luxury Day Trip

Around three hundred people each paid a fee of five hundred South African rand for a top-of-the-range 'Racing Fun Day' in July 1989. There would be a round trip from Johannesburg to Durban, an in-flight fashion show, a day at the races in their own marquee with entertainment and a slap-up luncheon with all the trimmings.

The fun started sooner than anyone had expected when the plane took off thirty minutes late and the flight was so bumpy that the fashion models could not walk straight. The marquee was pitched on waterlogged ground and there were no seats so everyone had to stand all day ankle-deep in water. The entertainers did not appear and, when the slap-up luncheon was served, racegoers who had not paid came in through slits in the canvas and ate all the food.

On the flight home the fun day's organiser felt he had to apologise when there was really no need.

The Worst Days Out

Anyone with our tastes seeking a good day out is advised to read those scholarly guides *Bollocks to Alton Towers* and *Far from the Sodding Crowd*, written by four inspiring young men who shun corporate theme parks and hi-tech interactive visitor experiences. Instead they guide us to tourist spots that 'require a little more effort and imagination (on occasion there is nothing to see at all)'. Their recommendations can hardly be faulted:

1. The Anaesthesia Heritage Centre is an excellent

museum dedicated to the history of anaesthetics. Exhibits offer a chance to see at first hand a fascinating Brady and Martin Spirometer, the Cardiff Penthrane Inhaler and the Newcastle Bang Ventilator. 'For a very thin slice of the population the artefacts on display are rich with bygone resonance.'

2. The Beckham Trail is an enthralling guided walk around Walthamstow visiting all those spots that were central to the footballer's early life. These include Whipps Cross Hospital where he was born and Walthamstow Stadium where he worked as a £10-a-night glass collector at greyhound races. The high point of the tour, for those with the energy for it after ten absorbing miles, is the visit to Gilwell Park where David went on cub camp.

3. The National Gas Museum has an unrivalled display of gas mangles, a small selection of gas irons and a copy of the iron collectors' magazine, *Pressing Matters*. There are, the authors write helpfully, only two push buttons in the whole museum, but 'one of them is arguably the most important button in Britain (after the one that launches Trident)'. It bears the simple label: 'Touch here to hear the Ascot Water Heater Song', performed by the Henry Hall Orchestra, whose previous hit was 'The Teddy Bears' Picnic'. It contains the catchy verse:

> Happy in the morning
> 'Cos the water is hot
> He can bath an Army
> The Ascot does the lot.

The authors inform us that they stayed pressing this button until the museum's closing time.

The Most Accident-Prone Person
in Scotland

The insurance company Accident Claims held a
competition in 2010 to find Scotland's most accident-
prone person. Whittling a hundred entries down
to three hugely impressive finalists, it appeared at
first to be a straight battle between Debbie Scott
from Aberdeen and the hot favourite, Douglas
McCorquodale of Perth.

Ms Scott was bitten by horses three times and,
furthermore, had so many fractures that she
became an expert, eventually getting a PhD in
bone and musculo-skeletal research. Meanwhile,
Mr McCorquodale knocked himself unconscious
falling out of his post van, burnt himself on holi-
day after covering himself with cooking oil instead
of suntan lotion and was banned from DIY by his
wife when he was crushed by a kitchen unit he had
just constructed. He is also known by name to staff
at the Accident & Emergency Unit at Perth Royal
Infirmary ever since he went in for an eye patch
after spraying himself with paint only to fall down a
hole on the way out. He hurt his arm and went back
in again for further treatment.

The eventual winner was the underdog, Lorraine
'Calamity' Crozier, who had been hospitalised on
twenty different occasions. In a varied career she
had fallen off a horse four times, crashed her

scooter and had a severe allergic reaction to a bubble bath. She was hit on the head by her daughter's swing in the park while receiving the mobile phone call announcing her victory.

The Worst Twelfth Night

The Twelfth Night of Christmas can so often be an anticlimax, spent quietly at home taking down the decorations, but the supreme master in this field is a Peterborough householder who turned it into a highly sociable once-in-a-lifetime event. In December 1992 he had taken down the Christmas tree lights and was storing them in the porch cupboard next to the gas and electricity meters. Inspiration struck and, because it was dark, he lit his cigarette lighter.

A magnificent jet of flame shot out and moments later the porch and the timber cladding of the house were ablaze, the electricity cable blew a hole in the gas main and the water pipe melted. He was certainly not short of company because ten firemen turned up on two fire engines and the gas, electricity and water officials arrived to dig up the front path and shut off the mains. Meanwhile, an electricity substation was closed, blacking out the entire neighbourhood. He and his partner spent the rest of Twelfth Night in bed and breakfast accommodation where they met even more people.

MOTORING NEWS

The Least Successful Lucky Charm

In August 1993 Tony Middlehurst, the editor of *Top Car* magazine, was given some lucky crystals. The effect was instant. Next morning the back door of his Vauxhall Cavalier burst open and scraped along a wall. Two days later, cruising down the motorway, he came to a screeching halt when bolts dropped from a bridge on the M2, cracking his windscreen and wrecking the bonnet. His car was finally written off in a collision with a lorry the following Tuesday, the same day that two test cars he was driving at work exploded.

After switching to a Citroën on Wednesday, Mr Middlehurst had a run-in with a van in a narrow street. Finally, on Thursday his replacement Vauxhall crashed into another van on a roundabout in south London. 'I've thrown the crystals away,' he told reporters.

The Murray Walker Lifetime Achievement Award

No one before or since has matched the gaffe-bejewelled motor-racing commentaries of Murray Walker, which were often more memorable than the race. Of his magnificently excitable delivery

Clive James once said: 'In his quieter moments he sounds as if his trousers are on fire.'

The following stand as a tribute to the great man's unforgettable life and work.

1. 'I don't make mistakes. I make prophecies which immediately turn out to be wrong.'
2. 'With half the race gone, there is half the race to go.'
3. Murray: 'So, Bernie, in the seventeen years since you bought McLaren, which of your many achievements do you think was the most important?'
   Bernie Ecclestone: 'Well, I don't remember buying McLaren.' (Mr Ecclestone used to own the Brabham team.)
4. 'Mansell is slowing it down, taking it easy. Oh no he isn't! It's a lap record.'
5. 'There's nothing wrong with the car except that it is on fire.'
6. Murray: 'There is a fiery glow coming from the back of the Ferrari.'
   James Hunt, co-commentator: 'No Murray, that's his rear safety light.'
7. 'Unless I'm very much mistaken . . . I AM very much mistaken.'

The Most Speeding Offences in One Go

Described as 'the world's most hapless driver', a motorist from Turkey set a new all-comers' record in November 2005 when he was flashed by the same speed camera four times in the space of one minute and thirty-seven seconds. Throughout this record-breaking run in the Swiss town of Kreuzlingen he had no idea he was passing a speed trap.

Baffled by the repeated flashing, he passed the spot again and again to investigate. This accomplished driver, whose identity was protected by Swiss privacy laws, told police that he thought someone was trying to annoy him with a flashgun and he wanted to check 'what was going on'.

His achievement was made possible by the location of two roundabouts on either side of the camera. Although speed cameras are designed to slow drivers down, this one had the opposite effect. Our man drove past at 36.6 mph, then 39, 42 and 47 mph. 'It was a feat requiring precision driving,' the police said.

The Worst Car

Asked by a national newspaper to name the worst motor car ever built, the motoring journalist David Burgess-Wise had no hesitation in acclaiming the Pennington Torpedo Auto Car of 1896. 'Every model designed by Edward Joel Pennington is worthy of being included in the list of the worst cars of all time,' he wrote, but this one has everything.

What makes any journey in this vehicle so exhilarating is not its three wheels or the fact that it has no bodywork and no suspension whatsoever. It is not the fact that it boasts throbbing cylinders right underneath the passenger seat with only nominal cooling so that everyone is kept exceptionally warm, particularly in the summer months. It is not that the driver sits on a bicycle saddle or that he steers with handlebars or that his forward view is obscured by three passengers sitting on a bench in front of him, or even that it has only a fast and slow gear and it is possible to engage both at once.

No, this car's unique world-beating quality is, according to Mr Burgess-Wise, that at high speeds it is virtually impossible to stop. But why would you want to stop a ride so memorable that it would remain with you always, waking or sleeping?

The Worst Car Thief in Russia

Even the Moscow police were impressed when they arrested Alexei Ashurin in September 2006. 'When we looked at his previous convictions we realised that he must be the most incompetent car thief in all Russia,' Captain Valery Buzovkin told reporters.

First, he was arrested after stealing a car and passing out drunk behind the wheel. Then he stole another car from outside a garage without realising it was there to have its brakes repaired. Minutes later he drove into a jeep while trying to stop at a red light.

On the latest occasion he was even more enterprising. Mr Ashurin was arrested while pushing a

Volkswagen along the road, having stopped what turned out to be a police car for assistance. 'He had run out of petrol, but as we pushed him we noticed a screwdriver sticking out of the ignition and that the lock was broken,' said Captain Buzovkin.

ALL AT SEA

The World Cruise that Went Nowhere

So many terrible things happen on world cruises (seasickness, day after day staring at the horizon out of the porthole, hurried day trips round Port Said fending off people selling postcards of their sister that are frankly distasteful). Only the legendary *Aurora* world cruise of 2005 avoided all of them.

Billed as a 'Grand Voyage', it was to be a 103-night cruise to forty ports in twenty-three countries, taking in Cape Verde and Easter Island, on the pride of the P&O fleet. Better still, the cruise in fact lasted eleven days, never lost sight of the English coast and the only port visited was Southampton.

Due to leave Southampton dock on 9 January, the *Aurora* developed engine problems so passengers were given free drink and top-notch on-ship entertainment. On 11 January it set sail and got as far as the Isle of Wight, which is well worth seeing actually, but then returned to Southampton. Passengers probably saw it with new eyes, having been away.

They were now told the engine would take six days to fix so they could leave the ship and visit at their leisure Southampton city centre, where nobody pesters you to have a ride on their overpriced camel.

On 17 January the *Aurora* sailed down the Solent as far as the Fawley oil refinery, which is an extraordinary sight with a very interesting history, and then back to Southampton again, of which one cannot get enough.

As darkness fell on 18 January passengers went on deck clutching free champagne to wave a reluctant goodbye to this fabled city. The band played. Flags flew. Passengers waved farewell. The *Aurora* did not move.

On 19 January, thoroughly rested by their cruise, 385 passengers decided to go home and left the ship, whereupon the *Aurora* set sail. The band played again. Flags et cetera. Everybody waved goodbye and the seventy-six-thousand-ton liner sailed out into the open sea, picked up speed and got as far as Devon where, opposite Start Point (have you been there? It's wonderful), the propulsion motor went phut and this fabulous cruise was cancelled. A spokesman for P&O said that passengers were 'sad' to leave the ship, which can be well imagined. There had not been one case of homesickness throughout the voyage.

The Least Successful Sea Rescue

Sailing from Sydney in 1829, the cutter *Mermaid* struck a reef in the Torres Straits and sank, leaving all twenty-two people on board clinging to a rock. Eventually they were rescued by another vessel, the *Swiftsure*, but a few days later it too was wrecked. Some hours after that, they were picked up by the *Governor Ready* with a cargo of timber and thirty-two people aboard. Three hours later it caught fire and everyone had to escape in lifeboats as the ship burned to the waterline.

When the *Comet* pulled alongside, its crew heard their story and decided that, all things considered, it might be best not to pick them up. With considerable difficulty their public-spirited captain persuaded his men to rescue the castaways. Seven days later the *Comet* sank in a sudden storm and the passengers, now accompanied by four separate crews, were rescued by the *Jupiter*.

In all four shipwrecks not a single life was lost, but the *Jupiter* struck the harbour at Port Raffles and was later scuttled when found to be beyond repair.

The Least Successful Ice Patrol

Set up in the late 1950s to combat the problems posed by icebergs to shipping in the Atlantic, the International Ice Patrol decided that the best approach was to destroy them all. Operated by the United States Coastguard, they first attempted to shoot the icebergs with machine guns. Apart from giving them an attractively pitted quality, this had no effect at all.

A decade later the whole enterprise got more serious and they decided to bomb the icebergs. Using twenty Second World War devices, they hoped to break the ice into smaller pieces. In fact, the icebergs proved shock-resistant and nothing happened.

At this point they moved on to thermite bombs, made from a powerful mixture of powdered aluminium and iron that explodes creating temperatures of several hundred degrees centigrade. The plan here was to break up and melt the icebergs in one impressive operation.

'It was absolutely spectacular,' said Captain Bob Dinsmore, commander of the patrol, 'but really didn't do anything to the icebergs.'

In a final moment of inspiration they tried to paint the icebergs black on the grounds that they would now absorb the sun's rays instead of reflecting them. This did work and some melted, but the Atlantic was now full of black paint which was as much of a problem for shipping as the icebergs. In his official report Captain Dinsmore said, 'Towards the elimination of icebergs we have tried everything we could think of, short of a nuclear bomb.' It was eventually decided to put up with the icebergs and find ways of steering round them.

☞ 7 ☜

MAINTAINING LAW AND ORDER

Inside the Criminal Mind

The Least Intimidating Bank Robber
The Least Successful Getaway
The Most Over-Enthusiastic Thieves
The Least Successful Attempt to Raid a Burger Bar
The Easiest Criminals to Catch
The Least Successful Break-In
The Importance of Having the Wrong Equipment

The Policing Role

The Least Successful Crime Deterrent
The Least Successful Undercover Operation
The Least Successful Crime Prevention Officer
The Least Successful Neighbourhood Watch
The Least Vigilant Police Force
The Least Effective Resocialisation Programme
The Most Badly Timed Police Raid

'Fiascos will always happen.'
LEONARD KAPINGA,
UN LESSONS LEARNED UNIT

The Least Intimidating Bank Robber

Understandably nervous before robbing his first bank, a top thief in Northampton relaxed himself with so much alcohol that he was unable to write his demand note. He staggered into a nearby shoe shop and asked the helpful women at the counter if they could possibly write one for him, reading 'Please hand over some money'.

He then stumbled off round the corner to the Nationwide Building Society and handed in his demand. They told him to go away because they were busy. Now at the top of his game and completely unstoppable, he went into two more banks, but fled the moment cashiers hit their alarm buttons.

Arrested for being drunk and disorderly, our man appeared before Judge Richard Bray at Northampton Crown Court in May 1995. 'This case is bizarre in the extreme,' the judge said. 'No one was in fear of you and you were not even arrested for the crimes you were trying to commit.'

The Least Successful Getaway

Escaping from Kirkham Open Prison in September 1994, a car thief made straight for the M6 and started hitching a lift. When a vehicle stopped he decided to confide in the motorist. 'I hope you don't mind but I'm an escaped prisoner,' he said.

'Not if you don't mind that I am a prison officer,' replied the driver, Steve Wynder, who immediately notified the police.

The Most Over-Enthusiastic Thieves

As part of their meticulous planning in March 2010, Albert Bailey and his sixteen-year-old accomplice telephoned the People's United Bank in Fairfield, Connecticut, to say they would be coming to rob it in about ten minutes so would they get out some bags of money?

This gave everybody plenty of time to get ready. The robbers arrived ten minutes later, as promised, and the sixteen-year-old was sent in with a note saying they had phoned earlier. The bank teller had $900 ready in a bag. Waiting outside, the police said the robbers could just have phoned them.

The Least Successful Attempt to Raid a Burger Bar

In November 1996 a thief walked into a branch of Burger King in Ypsilanti, Michigan, flashed a gun and demanded money. The shop assistant said he could not open the till without a food order. When the man ordered onion rings, the assistant said they were not available for breakfast. Frustrated, the thief left.

The Easiest Criminals to Catch

The greatest crimes are marked by an optimal simplicity that makes it possible to solve them almost immediately.

1. In January 1997 Michael Coulter was identified the second he stole trainers, three pairs of socks and some boxer shorts from a shop in Cookstown, County Tyrone. At seven foot five, he is Ireland's tallest man. 'Shop assistants noticed him immediately,' a spokesman for the Royal Ulster Constabulary said. 'He had to bend down coming in.'
2. A German robber burst into a Berlin bank with a pistol and screamed, 'Hand over the money!' Staff asked him if he wanted a bag, to which he replied: 'Damn right, it's a real gun!' Sensing that he was deaf, the manager set off the alarm. 'It was ridiculously loud, but he didn't seem to notice.' After five minutes, punctuated by our man occasionally shouting 'I'm a trained killer,' police

arrived and arrested him.

3. In March 2008 Ruben Zarate walked into a clothes shop in Chicago and demanded money. An employee told him that only the manager could open the safe, and he was not there. Mr Zarate then gave them his mobile phone number and asked if the manager could ring him when he got back. When he got the call, our chap returned, briefly repeated his demands and was taken straight to the police station.

4. Henry 'Headbanger' Smith was instantly identified as he fled the scene of his crime because he had his name tattooed across his forehead. Running away from a house in Gainsborough, Lincolnshire, with a stereo set hidden under a tea towel, he looked so suspicious that a taxi driver phoned the police. Mr Smith later said that his girlfriend did not like the stereo and threw it away.

The Least Successful Break-In

In November 1993 a glue sniffer broke into a glue factory in Brazil, but he lost all self-control when he saw his favourite and started inhaling directly from the vats. Overcome by fumes, he passed out, lost his balance and knocked over a vat of glue as he fell. By the time he came round he was stuck to the floor and had to lie there until staff turned up for work.

A police inspector said of the arrest: 'It took twelve of us, including eight firemen, to remove him and we had to take a dozen floorboards into custody as well.'

The Importance of Having the Wrong Equipment

In 1983 two men wearing balaclavas drove up to the State Bank in Melbourne, Australia. One stayed in the car with the engine running while the other jumped out clutching an enormous old doctor's bag and an equally large and old-fashioned double-barrelled, sawn-off shotgun with gigantic twin hammers.

He ran up to the door, tripped on the 'Welcome' mat, flew through the doorway, rolled into the bank and sprawled onto the floor. The gun hammers got trapped in the bag handle and he tried to pull them free, to no avail.

Everybody was watching this bravura performance with great interest as, cursing loudly, he tried kicking the gun loose. Finally in complete desperation, still lying on his back, he clasped the firearm and with both feet firmly pushed the bag away from the gun.

The bag was suddenly dislodged, causing the hammers to spring forward and discharge both barrels simultaneously into the bank's ceiling. Alarmed by the enormous bang, his accomplice rushed inside and dragged his colleague from the floor out to the waiting car, only to realise he had dropped his keys in the bank.

The Least Successful Crime Deterrent

Determined to reduce crime rates in Stockport, police put a life-size cardboard cut-out of PC Bob Molloy in the entrance of Sainsbury's. It was, according to vigilant observers, 'peeping out from behind the Creme Eggs'. In 2009 the cut-out was stolen by two women who were caught on CCTV. 'One held the door open, while the other ran out with the policeman under her arm,' a supermarket spokesman said.

Similar cut-outs used elsewhere in Stockport had also caused difficulties. 'It looked very realistic,' PC Molloy said. 'Just the other day someone told me that they had said hello to me in a store, but I never replied to them.'

The Least Successful Undercover Operation

In September 1994 undercover police closed in on a meeting of the ARM in the village hall at Cundall, Yorkshire, expecting to find the Animal Rights Militia planning their next outrage. In fact, they had surrounded a meeting of the Association of Radical Midwives.

When two women came out for a cigarette break, undercover detectives approached them and demanded to know what was going on. Encouraged by this male interest in progressive home-birth plans, the women filled them in. 'When we told them,' said Chris Warren, who organised the meeting, 'they just looked at each other and sneaked off. We had no idea what was going on outside or the panic we were causing.'

The Least Successful Crime Prevention Officer

In February 1990 police watching CCTV footage of a shoplifter immediately recognised him as their own crime prevention officer, stealing a pen and two pairs of tights. He was recorded in a store in the Sandwell Centre, West Bromwich, not far from Smethwick Police Station where he had recently been photographed by a local newspaper standing in front of a poster reading 'Watch out! There's a Thief About.'

The Least Successful Neighbourhood Watch

The least necessary Neighbourhood Watch was established in the early 1990s at the hamlet of Culbone in Somerset. The smallest parish in Britain, it had a population of twenty-three of whom twenty-one were deer. It is difficult enough to find Culbone, never mind finding somewhere to burgle there. Hidden in a remote valley on the other side of a moor and near the edge of a cliff, it is seven miles from the nearest town and reached by a dirt track.

The hamlet contained only two cottages, which were at the time inhabited by Dennis and Barry. One day, Dennis announced that he was setting up a Neighbourhood Watch. Given that Dennis would be running the scheme, this meant that Barry would be under day-long surveillance as the only realistic suspect. This was hardly necessary because Barry had no electricity and no car and showed no interest whatever in buying consumer durables, let alone stealing them.

The Least Vigilant Police Force

Every year police from three neighbouring Australian states meet to vote for the winner of the Knacker Award, which is given annually to the police officer who has committed the biggest blunder. In 1989 they took the unprecedented step of giving this award to the entire Renmark police force after the town was visited by a sixteen-stone conman.

This stranger was so amiable that the townspeople showered him with kindness. A local bank gave him a cheque account on which he wrote $15,000-worth of dud cheques. The local gym even gave him free exercise sessions which enabled him to lose just over a stone. On the day he left, his truck broke down. A motorist who stopped to help saw three colour television sets and three video recorders in the back and called the police.

The man reassured police that the merchandise was his. Once again nothing was too much trouble. They towed him back to town, had his truck repaired and even found him overnight accommodation. Next morning he thanked them profusely and left. They did not see him again until several days later, while watching a TV crime programme, *Australia's Most Wanted*, in which he was heavily featured as the subject of a nationwide manhunt.

The Least Effective Resocialisation Programme

As part of a 'resocialisation programme' for long-term prisoners in January 1990, Robert Walters was allowed out of Collins Bay Penitentiary in Canada accompanied by his probation guard. Having served half of his twenty-four-year sentence for robbery, he was taken into town for six hours so that he could re-acclimatise to normal life.

The guard drove Mr Walters into nearby Kingston and they went to a hotel so that he could re-acclimatise himself to having an alcoholic drink. He then re-acclimatised himself to having a second and then a third. Eventually he told his guard, who was also thoroughly enjoying the afternoon, that he was going to pop out for a minute. He returned soon afterwards with thousands of dollars stuffed down his trousers.

Sitting in their car outside the hotel, the guard was arrested for driving under the influence of alcohol, while Mr Walters was arrested for re-acclimatising himself to robbing the Royal Bank of Canada.

The Most Badly Timed Police Raid

On Thursday 27 November 2008 the burglar alarm went off at the PNC Bank in Montgomery Township, New Jersey. At 8.40 p.m. police cars raced to the scene. The bank was closed and its blinds were drawn, but officers caught a glimpse of a menacing and shadowy figure inside.

First they called out the SWAT team, who take this sort of thing very seriously. They arrived with heavy body armour, ballistic shields, entry tools, advanced night-vision optics, motion detectors, sub-machine guns, shotguns and sniper rifles.

This elite squad sealed off the entire area and evacuated residents from three nearby apartment buildings. Then they used loudhailers and telephones to make contact with whoever might be inside the building, but got no response.

After two hours the SWAT team decided to storm

the bank. Shortly after 10.20 p.m., with a helicopter hovering overhead and camera crews arriving from all over the state, they finally gained entry.

The shadowy figure was a cardboard cut-out of a salesman offering low-cost finance deals to customers.

8

AN EVERYDAY STORY OF MEDIA FOLK

The Least Successful TV Interview
The Worst Ballroom Dancer
The Least Successful Political Newsflash
The Least Successful Documentary
The Least Successful Thought for the Day
The Worst TV Surprise
The Worst Oscar Triumph
The Least Successful Top Secret
The Least Successful Breakfast Show
The John Motson Lifetime Achievement Award
The Least Convincing Moral High Ground
The Least Successful TV Channel Launch
The Least Successful Branding Campaign
The Least Exciting Live Broadcast
The Least Successful Live Radio Interview
The Importance of Wrong Answers

'What are you working on?'
'I'm preparing my next mistake.'
BERTOLT BRECHT, *Stories of Mr Keuner*

The Least Successful TV Interview

Guy Goma moved from the Congo to Britain for a job in information technology. This decision was thoroughly vindicated in May 2006 when he arrived at BBC Television Centre to be interviewed for a job as an IT assistant. In the waiting room with him was Guy Kewney, a distinguished IT consultant, who was waiting to go on live TV.

Someone arrived and asked Mr Goma if he was here for the interview and duly led him through to the studio. He should have smelt a rat when he noticed the TV cameras and the fact that they started applying make-up to his face. There are, however, cultural differences between the Congo and Britain and it was reasonable to assume that this was one of them.

The interview started and the BBC's Karen Bowerman introduced him as 'Guy Kewney, head of Newswireless.net'. Mr Goma was visibly surprised, but gamely answered the questions.

'With regards to the costs involved, do you think now more people will be downloading online?' asked the interviewer. The question itself was routine, mundane even, but Mr Goma's answer thrilled all who saw it.

'Actually,' he said, 'if you can go everywhere you're gonna see a lot of people downloading to the internet and the website, and everything they want. But I think it is much better for the development and . . . uh . . . to inform people what they want and to get the easy way and so faster if they are looking for.'

Afterwards he had his real interview. It lasted ten minutes and he did not get the job, but by then he was a national TV star and too busy discussing his inspired television appearance on GMTV, ITV, Channel 4 and the BBC itself.

The Worst Ballroom Dancer

The outstanding ballroom dancer of his generation, John Sergeant was invited to appear on *Strictly Come Dancing*, the BBC's celebrity cavort-and-caper contest. With odds of 100–1 to win, and only known hitherto as a serious political journalist, he was enormously promising from the start.

In no time he was doing some staggeringly beautiful moves. No one who saw it will ever forget his paso doble in full Mexican rig. Dragging his partner across the floor 'like a sack of potatoes' while stamping his feet, he made the occasional surging trot with a fixed lugubrious expression that hovered between concentration and the most magnificent boredom.

The panel of studio judges were quick to see his vast potential: 'His posture is wrong, his feet are turned in, he hasn't got the rise and fall, his head's on one side. In terms of dance, everything is wrong with it.' They also pointed out that while other performers were constantly practising, John sat and read the *Guardian*. 'We've never had anyone this bad who has gone this far.'

Week after week increasingly shirty judges placed him last only to be overruled by the adoring public, who voted to keep him on the show. 'As time went on, it became increasingly obvious that I might win,' he said. 'That is a frightening thought for me.' His odds fell to 10–1.

When he announced his resignation from the contest, the BBC was instantly flooded with complaints. There was a massive press conference, a report on the national TV news and a week-long newspaper debate over whether his complete lack of rhythm and skills should be any bar to his continuation in the contest. Lord Mandelson, the secretary of state for industry, broke off from government business to say, 'He should not bow out. He has become the People's John Travolta.'

There was such uproar that Mr Sergeant was invited to dance a farewell waltz that stole the show. He won a long standing ovation.

The next series contained his only genuine rival, Ann Widdecombe MP. As one judge put it, she has 'two left feet, is three quarters bosom and dances like a tugboat pulling the *Ark Royal* up the Clyde'.

One critic enthused: 'The producers put her on last so you were forced to watch the really good dancers as a sort of boring canapé before you got the gorgeous main course.'

Miss Widdecombe said she wanted to 'fly like Dumbo' when she danced the tango. She became the first contestant to be lifted off the floor in a harness.

'I turned down *Strictly* six times. I didn't think I could do it,' she told reporters. 'Then I saw John Sergeant. He broke the mould.'

The Least Successful Political Newsflash

Faced with a challenge to her leadership of the Conservative Party in 1990, the prime minister, Margaret Thatcher, made a wholly characteristic announcement: 'I fight on. I fight to win.' This would be of no interest to specialists like us except that BBC Radio 4 seized the moment for some trailblazing journalism.

She stood in a ballot that was counted only minutes before the deadline for the next news bulletin. Wisely the political correspondent recorded two reports, one announcing her outright victory and the other her resignation.

To their credit, they broadcast the wrong one despite her narrow victory. Days later she stood in a second ballot and lost, which only enhanced the BBC's reputation for being first with the news.

The Least Successful Documentary

In May 1994 the BBC commissioned a documentary entitled *A Country Wedding* for its distinguished series *40 Minutes*. For six months they filmed a happy rural couple discussing their relationship, their hopes and plans, the reason why they had opted for an October wedding, their views on children, their extensive plans for the reception, how the guests were chosen, the importance of shared decisions, the whole question of floral bouquets and how they hoped to combine her career as a globetrotting violinist with his stay-at-home interest in running a fishing business.

They had thirty hours of television in the can when the wedding was called off and the engagement cancelled. The producers then changed the programme's title to *A Year on a Country Estate*. They had just re-edited the extensive footage, and everybody was very excited, when the *40 Minutes* series was axed. In a world where there is far too much media and a surfeit of information they did the decent thing and the documentary was never shown.

The Least Successful Thought for the Day

A seasoned broadcaster, Rabbi Lionel Blue had his finest hour on BBC Radio 4's *Thought for the Day*. Live on air, he turned the first page of his uplifting talk only to find that he had brought not page two, as lesser souls might have done, but a duplicate of page one.

Seizing his chance, the maestro electrified his audience: he hummed and hawed, paused and fluffed, stumbled and floundered and all to the very highest quality. 'I muffed it,' he said later. 'I thought, "Thank God I'm leaving for Canada."'

When he got back a few weeks later he found the biggest and most enthusiastic mailbag he had ever received.

The Worst TV Surprise

The late, great broadcaster Eamonn Andrews was best known for launching the TV series *This Is Your Life*. Each week the plan was to make a famous person very surprised when Mr Andrews arrived unexpectedly with a Big Red Book containing their life story. The celebrity was then dragged into the studio to meet all his relatives and long-lost friends, whether he wanted to or not.

In 1972 one programme featured a stand-up comedian called Charlie Williams, who was appearing at a theatre in Batley. The plan was for Mr Andrews to walk onto the stage with the big red book as his act was finishing. Because he was such a well-known celebrity in his day, they had to keep him hidden in order to preserve the surprise. He took cover outside the stage door in a narrow space behind a large, rusty fence of corrugated iron held off the ground by two wooden supports.

Then a man came out and began urinating endlessly through a space at the bottom of the corrugated iron, all over Mr Andrews's feet, filling his shoes and soaking his socks. 'His relief seemed to go on a very long time,' the programme's producer recalled. The famous presenter could not move or say anything: the surprise would have been wrecked.

No sooner had the man finished than someone whispered that the act was coming to an end. The producer said he would never forget how Mr Andrews's shoes squelched as he walked across the stage, nor the greater than usual surprise of his celebrity victim.

The Worst Oscar Triumph

In 1983 Zbigniew Rybczyński won an Oscar for Best Animated Short Film, but things soon started to pick up. For a start, the award's presenter, Kristy McNichol, mispronounced his name when announcing him as the winner, but the evening really got into its stride when his acceptance speech was cut off by the orchestra.

He then nipped outside for a cigarette and the security guard would not let him back in. Misinterpreting his fine Polish accent and uncertain

English, the guard assumed he was drunk. 'I have Oscar! I have Oscar!' yelled Mr Rybczyński, who was now pinned against a wall. Rounding off a perfect occasion, he fought back, but was led off and spent the night in jail relaxing while everything was sorted out.

The Least Successful Top Secret

With the Falklands War reaching a critical stage in May 1982, British troops launched a top-secret assault on Goose Green. Moving under cover of darkness, a regiment of paratroopers set up a hidden encampment and lay in wait.

Taking the enemy completely by surprise, the BBC World Service broadcast our people's exact whereabouts to, among other places, the Falklands. 'I was just in total disbelief,' said Captain Malcolm Worsley-Tonks. 'I just thought, "That won't happen. Nobody is going to be that ridiculous."' The Argentinians also heard it, reached the same conclusion and decided it was a trick. Truth is the first casualty of war, but not, happily, on this occasion.

The Least Successful Breakfast Show

Early-morning radio is full of bright and breezy disc jockeys whose irritating chirpiness only makes things worse. Showing a rare and wonderful consideration for his listeners in June 1998, the breakfast-show host on the Sunderland radio station, Sun FM, set a new high-water mark when he fell asleep for thirty minutes during his own broadcast. Oh the peace. Oh the calm. Suddenly there was time to reflect, to muse and to collect one's thoughts for the day ahead. He was woken up by his boss at 7.30.

'One minute I was sitting there reading my advert list – the next I had him shouting at me to wake up,' he said. Tragically for the people of Sunderland this pioneering and humane DJ was replaced by a more conventionally raucous creature.

The John Motson Lifetime Achievement Award

There have been many perfectly adequate football commentators, but only John Motson has really explored the possibilities of surrealism. Like all surrealist art, his work features the element of surprise, unexpected juxtapositions and non sequitur. He has won the admiration of football fans everywhere.

1. 'For those of you watching in black and white, Spurs are in the all-yellow strip.'
2. 'In a sense it's a one-man show . . . except that there are two men involved, Hartson and Berkovic, and a third man, the goalkeeper.'

3. 'Just one minute of overtime so you can put the eggs on now if you like.'
4. 'Bruce has got the taste of Wembley in his nostrils.'
5. 'What a time to score . . . twenty-seven minutes!'
6. 'The goals made such a difference to the way this game went.'
7. 'Hold on to your cups and glasses . . . You can smash them now. David Beckham has scored.'

The Least Convincing Moral High Ground

In January 1997 a poll showed two thirds of Church of England vicars could not list the Ten Commandments. Taking a stern view on this, the *Independent* put these clergymen straight and listed all ten. It got two of them wrong, omitting the fourth commandment completely ('Remember the Sabbath day, to keep it holy') and introducing a new and very important free-standing commandment ('Thou shalt not covet thy neighbour's house'), perhaps in timely response to a contemporary interest in property prices.

The Least Successful TV Channel Launch

While waiting to launch its new science-fiction channel in 1994, a cable TV company in Columbia, South Carolina, decided to point a camera at a tank and broadcast some fabulous tropical fish swimming in circles for fourteen hours a day. At least it would fill the space, they reckoned, while the creatives got everything ready.

Eventually the new channel was launched with great fuss and fanfare. The company was flooded with calls from angry viewers who said it was not as interesting as the fish and demanded to know when they were coming back. Bowing to public pressure, they put this marvellous tank on another channel, where it continues to broadcast fourteen hours a day to great public acclaim.

The Least Successful Branding Campaign

The very latest branding idea from Saatchi & Saatchi in New Zealand was their 'Our Auckland Big A' campaign. The idea was to foster civic pride in that fine city by encouraging residents to greet each other with a signal in the form of an 'A' made by joining the thumbs and fingers of both hands.

The campaign was abandoned in March 2001 when they received complaints from the Deaf Association of New Zealand and various women's groups saying it was not only the internationally recognised sign for 'vagina', but also very like the sign-language symbol for Aids.

The Least Exciting Live Broadcast

In a TV first, *Police Action Live* promised 'an extraordinary two-hour programme showing policing as it happens'. The plan was to have real-time footage of the events of one evening in November 1995 that would switch between a vice patrol in Manchester, a foot patrol in Northumbria, a policewoman answering 999 calls at Scotland Yard and the custody suite at Charing Cross police station.

'For the next two hours,' said the presenter, Dermot Murnaghan, 'you are going to witness police action as you've never seen it before.'

For 120 minutes nothing happened at all.

Having explained that there were satellites involved in all this, Mr Murnaghan then said he was going to 'criss-cross the country'. He found the Manchester vice squad touring deserted backstreets with no vice anywhere. WPC Doreen Davies in 'the pursuit car' at Trafalgar Square was stuck in traffic and inaudible due to her siren. In Newcastle two coppers on the beat could not make themselves heard above drunken lads shouting at the camera. 'Quite a potty there for Constables Speedy and Charlton,' observed the presenter, who probably meant to say 'posse'.

Even when the police did arrest a single, solitary drunk the cameras could not show him for legal reasons and dwelt upon his trousered bottom as the duty officer did the paperwork. After fifty-eight minutes the only police action we had seen was a traffic constable advising motorists to join the AA.

'Right,' said Mr Murnaghan. 'We're going to Hampshire now where our traffic police are in a high-speed chase.' 'Yeah, Dermot,' said the reporter, 'not quite a chase.' They were driving to a lay-by to await a possibly suspicious vehicle from Wiltshire. It failed to arrive.

The Least Successful Live Radio Interview

On 11 December 2010, BBC Radio 4 telephoned Michael Crockart MP, a junior member of government, saying they had a slot on *The World at One* in seven minutes' time. Would he give his views on student fee increases? Having the wrong number in their contact book, they got through to Paul Leatherbarrow, a twenty-seven-year-old construction worker, who was having tea on a building site. 'They asked if I was willing to go on the radio. I said I was.'

Recalling this bold attempt to broaden public access to the airwaves, Mr Leatherbarrow said: 'There were twelve of us in the tea cabin at work. I went outside and my mates put the radio on. I was just told to hold until I heard the presenter talking to me. When I answered, all my mates were banging on the window saying, "It's you. It's you."'

The interviewer, James Naughtie, got straight down to business. 'Are you going to resign over this one?' he asked.

Making no bones about it, Mr Leatherbarrow said that he was, indeed, 'prepared to resign'.

Mr Naughtie asked: 'Meaning you would like to vote against this, but you feel you can't, and therefore you will resign in order to do so?'

Mr Leatherbarrow answered: 'If I'm backed into a corner, yeah. I mean the main thing, what was the big problem from the beginning, was the grit bins.'

He had here introduced the very important subject of grit bin shortages in icy conditions. This matter rarely gets adequate airtime in the metropolitan media, but was a subject close to the heart of his mates in the tea cabin. At that point the line went dead.

'I think we've lost Michael Crockart,' said Mr Naughtie. 'So I'm going to go now to our political correspondent, Iain Watson, who is at Westminster.' They analysed the interview and saw 'significant' evidence of 'growing cracks' within the party.

Later in the afternoon the London *Evening Standard* ran a story saying: 'Nick Clegg, the Deputy Prime Minister, was engulfed in a full-scale crisis over tuition fees today as one of his Liberal Democrat MPs vowed to resign from the coalition government rather than abandon his morals.'

'Resigning probably will be the only option,' said

Mr Leatherbarrow, whose opinion had hardened during the afternoon. 'There are so many just prepared to sway from left to right, and up and down, on the command of other people. You can't keep doing this.'

This was not the first time that he had been contacted as the MP. 'A couple of weeks ago I got a call for Mr Crockart saying my dinner date was confirmed and did I want pork?' Mr Leatherbarrow said pork would be fine so long as it was well done.

The Importance of Wrong Answers

The most memorable contestant ever to appear on *Who Wants to Be a Millionaire?* was Michelle Simmonds, a hotel clerk from Luton, who in February 2001 went home with no money at all and left the country when the programme was broadcast.

The first round traditionally brings a simple question designed to ensure no one leaves empty-handed. Mrs Simmonds thoroughly challenged this concept when asked which of the following was composed by Johann Sebastian Bach: Was it (A) 'Air on a G String', (B) 'Breeze in a Bikini', (C) 'Waft in the Y-fronts' or (D) 'Gust up the Gusset'? To her credit, she needed help.

Her finest hour came when she was asked which word links a type of mammal with an archbishop. 'Is it (A) "Carnivore", (B) "Rodent", (C) "Primate" or (D) "Marsupial"?' She toyed briefly with the correct answer of 'Primate', but rightly dismissed it as ridiculous and settled at the last minute for 'Marsupial'. 'I can't believe you've done that,' said the show's host, Chris Tarrant, who has all the answers in front of him and so finds it easy. When Mrs Simmonds explained that she could not imagine calling an archbishop a primate, Mr Tarrant replied: 'You don't call him a marsupial. Put it that way.'

☞ 9 ☜

THE SHOW MUST GO ON

The Least Successful Stage Set
The Least Successful Prompter
The Least Appropriate Musical
The Least Successful Concert
The Least Satisfactory Circus
The Worst Eurovision Song Contest Entry
The Musical that Closed before It Opened
The Worst Snow White and the Seven Dwarfs
The Least Successful Children's Film Show
The Least Successful Film-Launch Stunt

Homage to Ed Wood

The Worst Film Director
The Worst Scriptwriter
The Worst Film

'My reputation grows with every failure.'
GEORGE BERNARD SHAW

The Least Successful Stage Set

Never have the possibilities of a sloping stage been more innovatively explored than in a celebrated Wexford Opera Festival performance of Spotini's *La vestale* in 1979, set in a vestal virgin's temple. They took the exciting decision to cover the floor with Formica, which not only looks like marble, but also has the added attraction of acute and liberating slipperiness. The plan was to cover the stage with lemon juice so the cast's feet would stick to the floor.

According to Wexford legend, a cleaning lady was so professionally affronted by the state of this stage that she washed and polished it one afternoon, helping to create the most inventive and free-range choreography seen on the operatic stage for a hundred years.

The curtain rose. Making a magnificent entrance, the Roman general Licinio strode onto the stage, fell flat on his back and slithered towards the footlights. Singing throughout, he got to his feet. After several plucky attempts to walk back upstage, he decided to stay where he was, no doubt calculating that the next character to enter, his friend Cinna, would shortly be joining him near the footlights anyway.

On came Cinna, arms waving, who hurtled down the stage and crashed into his chum at speed. The script demands that they 'embrace in a friendly greeting', which they amply fulfilled, being locked in each other's arms as they were propelled towards the orchestra pit.

Averting disaster at the last second, they worked their way gingerly along the edge of the stage 'like mountaineers seeking a route round an unbridge-able crevasse', according to the opera critic Bernard Levin, who looked on with a growing delight.

Still singing and clutching onto each other, the pair decided to make for a pillar bearing the sacred vestal flame that was three feet further up and embedded firmly in the stage floor.

At this point matters were considerably improved by the entrance of the chorus.

Throwing themselves into their roles, they also decided to make for the fixed pillar, which was now becoming quite crowded. Happily, this chorus of centurions, gladiators and vestal virgins decided to form 'a daisy chain of mutual support', according to Mr Levin, leading from the pillar across the stage with everyone clutching on to each other until they were all accommodated. The audience was so moved by this performance that most were weeping and some struggled for breath.

With impeccable improvisation the heroine herself, the priestess Giulia, skated into the wings and kicked her shoes off. Finding on her return that this did not improve things, she slithered back into the wings and removed her tights as well.

The act ends with 'extended triumphal dances', which have rarely been more memorable.

The Least Successful Prompter

Coming from a theatrical family, Jason Connery had the benefit of tremendously sound acting advice when young. His mother, the actress Diane Cilento, had told him about the importance of dramatic pauses to give himself a more expansive stage persona. He put this to excellent use in his memorable performance in the Gordonstoun School Drama Society production of *The Pilgrim's Progress*.

On he came as the monster Apollyon, covered in fish scales and wonderfully ferocious. He was doing some of these dramatic pauses to powerful effect, except that every time he paused the prompter jumped in and shouted out his line. The monster got more and more annoyed until eventually he ran over to the wings and whopped him. Knocked off balance and sent flying, the prompter fell off his stool and dropped the prompt book.

This outstanding young actor had just run back and growled a bit more when he forgot his words.

The prompter, now on the floor with his book closed, was unable to find the line. The happy result was an absolutely perfect pause, full, rich and resonant, that was long enough to satisfy even his mother.

The Least Appropriate Musical

Acclaimed by critics as 'tosh', 'doomed' and 'a triumph of tastelessness', *The Fields of Ambrosia* was so special that in February 1996 its producers offered to give people their money back if they left after the first act. In fact, no one took up this offer because everyone had heard about the awesome final scene where – after multiple onstage slayings – the hero, an executioner, is strapped into his own electric chair. Singing 'Give me a send-off that lights up the party,' he ascends into heaven with his recently electrocuted girlfriend, both of them wearing ball gowns.

'I've been twice,' Dave from Hornchurch told newspaper reporters. 'It's the worst thing I've ever seen. I've told all my friends to come. Have you seen the ending yet? It's staggering.'

The musical was written by a 'young insomniac composer' called Martin Silvestri and the actor-librettist Joel Higgins, having decided, quite rightly, that a story about an executioner who travels through the deep south of America with his mobile electric chair was very good material for a musical. 'One minute you're here, the next you're gone – thanks to the comfy chair you're sitting on' was just one of the show-stopping lyrics.

Obviously backers rushed to pour money into a show of this calibre. After 'tryouts in various hotels' it opened at the Aldwych Theatre in London's star-studded West End. Critics were particularly struck by a scene in which the chorus of jailbirds were molested by warders waving truncheons.

The Least Successful Concert

Commissioned in 1749, Handel's *Music for the Royal Fireworks* exceeded all expectations in its first performance. Artisans and pyrotechnicians were summoned from all over Europe for the spectacle. The supervisor of stage design at the Paris Opéra was enlisted to construct an immense Doric temple in London's Green Park to house the display. Complete with steps, pillars and passageways, the 410-foot-long building boasted a hundred cannons, a bas-relief of George II and a two-hundred-foot pole bearing an allegorical representation of the sun.

Drawn by the promise of fireworks, a large crowd gathered, and they were not disappointed. Fireworks immediately ignited several fires across the park, the temple burned to the ground and swords were drawn among the organisers. Handel himself observed afterwards that 'creativity is best avoided'.

The Least Satisfactory Circus

Admirers still speak very highly of Bob's Circus in the 1950s. In an article headlined 'The Worst Circus Ever', the *Legends of the Midwest* magazine wrote: 'Never before has a worse circus travelled from small town to small town. A stripeless zebra turned out to be a large dog and lion trainers were actually children in a cage with two domestic cats to make them look bigger.'

All of this, however, pales in comparison to the touring circus that arrived in the Belarusian city of Vitebsk in January 2011 with a 'New Year Spectacular'.

Posters had been up all week promising 'jugglers, midgets, fantasy heroes, exotic animals' and an unforgettable finale. Black bears were mentioned along with performing crocodiles, monkeys and real orcs.

Local media pointed out that orcs are fictional goblins, but this did not stop thousands of tickets being snapped up.

At the first and last performance on 2 January there were no black bears, only one exotic animal, a complete dearth of midgets and, more to the point, not a single orc. The artistes kept falling off their bicycles and the jugglers repeatedly dropped their props. 'They had a few poodles and one crocodile,' said Igor Kalmuk, who was in the audience.

It became the first circus in recorded history where the audience called the police and insisted the performers were breathalysed. 'How else can you explain that one of them fell off his bike three times in two minutes?' one spectator asked *Komsomolskaya Pravda*.

During the memorable finale the police arrived and tested the artistes. As it turned out, they were all sober.

Afterwards Mr Kalmuk went in person to see the circus administrator. She said the animals had got 'stopped at customs' and the orcs were 'outside Moscow'.

A spokesman for the Belarusian police said an investigation was underway into whether a crime had been committed and, if so, what it was.

The Worst Eurovision Song Contest Entry

Norway is the undisputed leader in the Eurovision Song Contest. It has not only come last ten times, which is the record, but also attained a grand slam of four 'nul points' so far. These Eurovision thoroughbreds have not necessarily produced the most memorable individual performance, however.

The most spectacular nought ever scored in the entire competition was achieved by our very own British entry, 'Cry Baby', in 2003. Writing in *Nul Points*, a book celebrating all who have scored nought in this competition, Tim Moore describes it as 'The worst noise heard on a Eurovision stage in the contest's forty-seven-year history'.

Even *The Eurovision Song Contest – the Official History* describes it as 'the least successful entry in the history of the contest so far', not least because it was the first to score nought points from the enlarged entry of twenty-six countries.

The Liverpool pop duo Jemini gave a marvellous performance. They both cavorted with impressive abandon and their unique sound was glowingly described by music reviewers as 'off key'.

This was put down to the fact that they could not hear the backing track due to technical difficulties. After their triumph Chris Comby, a member of the duo, said: 'It was one of the best performances we've ever done. It was the performance of a lifetime.'

The Musical that Closed before It Opened

The legendary 1966 musical version of *Breakfast at Tiffany's* has the unique distinction of closing before its opening night because the producer did not wish to 'subject critics and the public to an excruciatingly boring evening'. The exciting thing about this show was that it never gelled. Far too many things do gel, but not this. How was it done?

The central act of genius was changing the main character, Holly Golightly, from the promiscuous wild child of Truman Capote's novella to a sweet-natured virgin and then, later on, to a hard-drinking prostitute.

By the time the librettist had written good-time songs for a wayward, conniving minx, Holly had the home life of a nun. Playing the part was Mary Tyler Moore, an actress much loved as a winsomely sweet and ideal TV wife. Among the songs she now had to sing were the raunchy 'Good Girls Go to Heaven, Bad Girls Just Go Everywhere' and 'Hot Damn'. The director, meanwhile, was spending hours at the dentist for major reconstructive surgery and could not speak to sort it all out.

There was no second act so this was written as they went along. Eventually, it was decided that the whole script should be rewritten. Holly was now turned into a right doxy and critics in Philadelphia were appalled at the sight of Mary Tyler Moore swearing like an enraged dockyard navvy.

Having sacked two directors and two librettists and thrown out the original script and score, the producer, David Merrick, asked the playwright Edward Albee to do another rewrite.

'They had made a perfectly safe, middlebrow, mediocre and, I thought, extremely boring musical that would probably run a year on Broadway,' Mr Albee said. 'I managed to turn it into a disaster that never opened.'

The director was upset by the new script and left, saying it was not his kind of show. In the meantime Mr Albee decided he did not think much of it either and started again.

After all the changes, including the introduction of several fantasy sequences, the show was now a serious musical drama that opened with the character of Mag Wildwood delivering a searing soliloquy in which she ended up stretched out and sobbing on the stage.

It lasted four fabulous hours. After four preview performances the producer decided that this show had reached its peak and disappointingly pulled the plug.

The Worst Snow White and the Seven Dwarfs

Inundated with complaints after the Christmas 2004 production of *Snow White and the Seven Dwarfs*, the Altmark theatre in Stendal, Germany, wished to make it clear that due to budgetary constraints they could only afford four dwarfs.

Susanne Kreuzer, the theatre spokeswoman, said,

'We are a small theatre company so we've attached two puppets in dwarf costumes to the back of a wall. The actor who plays the Prince sometimes gets on his knees and joins the end of the line, but he can only do that when he is not playing his role.'

Asked by children why there were sometimes only six dwarfs on stage, the inventive Ms Kreuzer replied: 'The seventh one was stuck down the mine, working overtime.'

The Least Successful Children's Film Show

A Saturday morning film show for children at the Connaught Theatre in Worthing ended in uproar in March 1998. It was found that the projectionist had shown not *The Rainbow*, starring Bob Hoskins, a film about four children and a dog who travel to a magical rainbow, but Ken Russell's *The Rainbow*, based on a steamy novel by D. H. Lawrence.

'It was all right for the first ten minutes and then they started swearing and stripping off,' said Michelle Provette, who had brought her son Jamie and nine of his friends as a seventh birthday treat. This was one of three birthday parties in the audience, all looking forward to seeing Bob Hoskins and the dog.

'I was gobsmacked by what we saw,' said Mrs Provette, who went on to describe 'lesbian love-making, effing and blinding and full frontal nudity'. In due course a detachment of irate parents stormed into the foyer and surrounded the house manager.

'Eventually one of the dads got up, clapped his hands and suggested everyone should leave.'

The Least Successful Film-Launch Stunt

At the New York premiere of Walt Disney's film *Pinocchio* in 1940 the studio wanted to do something a little bit special. For that reason, eleven dwarfs in Pinocchio costumes were sent to prance and cavort all day on top of the cinema's front canopy. As a gesture of encouragement, alcohol was sent up at lunchtime and by three in the afternoon 'all eleven dwarfs were on the roof, drunk, naked, belching and playing cards'. The police came with ladders and took them away in pillowcases. They really knew how to launch a family picture in those days.

HOMAGE TO ED WOOD

'Learn to see bad films.
They are sometimes sublime.'
ADO KYROU, *Le Surréalisme au cinéma*

The Worst Film Director

Ed Wood is one of the all-time greats and a genius in our field. So many film directors are afflicted with divine discontent, which is a bore for everyone else, but Ed Wood was completely satisfied with everything he did. It is so important to be happy in your work and no matter how many lines were fluffed nor how many props fell over, he hardly ever asked for a retake.

A transvestite with an angora fetish, Mr Wood filmed thirty scenes a day when most directors attempt only one. He never gave the actors direction or discussed the motivation of their characters. This was partly because he had no idea what their motivation was and partly because he was too busy rushing around shouting 'More smoke, more smoke.' He just wanted the actors to say their lines, which is why there is such a wonderful blankness on everyone's face when anyone else is speaking.

This exquisite artist had a God-given lack of self-awareness which made the whole thing possible. His unique working method involved alternating newly filmed action with stock library footage that had nothing to do with the story. In *Glen or Glenda* (1953), his seminal film about cross-dressing, the hero, played by Mr Wood himself, is explaining to his partner, Barbara, why her angora sweater keeps disappearing. He chose this moment to insert footage of a buffalo stampede. Upon this was superimposed Bela Lugosi sitting in an armchair, impersonating the puppet master of all humanity, declaiming: 'Pull the strings! Pull the strings! A mistake is made. A story must be told.'

He was the first director to use symbolism with objects standing in for the special effects he would have liked to be able to afford. In this way a photographic enlarger became an atomic death-ray machine and the ever present shower curtain served as anything from a busy police station to an aeroplane cockpit.

His reputation rests upon six films including *Night of the Ghouls* (1959), a horror film that is blessedly free from horror, in which mute expressionless actors watch a trumpet floating visibly on strings while a grimacing man in a pith helmet speaks in slow motion. *Bride of the Monster* (1955) stars Lugosi as a mad doctor who becomes an atomic superman. He deflects police gunfire by pulling faces and fights with a flaccid rubber octopus stolen from Republic Studios.

To produce work of this calibre Mr Wood gathered around him a magnificent entourage who formed his acting troupe. There was Tor Johnson, a four-hundred-pound wrestler who regularly broke Mr Wood's toilet seat and later became famous as a latex Halloween mask. He was joined by the splendid Vampira, a TV horror film show host, who dressed like an Addams Family dominatrix mermaid. The line-up also included Criswell, the flamboyantly inaccurate psychic, as himself (see Chapter 10).

Echoing Brecht and anticipating Jean-Luc Godard, Mr Wood reminds us that 'this is only a movie, not real life'. Ignoring the tropes of classical narrative style, he triumphed over all obstacles including his own lack of conventional ability. The 1996 edition of *Cult Flicks and Trash Pics* said of Mr Wood's *Plan 9 from Outer Space* (1959), 'The film has become so famous for its own badness that it is beyond criticism.'

To appreciate Mr Wood's genius as a scriptwriter, see below.

The Worst Scriptwriter

A Renaissance man, Ed Wood both directed and acted in his films. Prudently, he also wrote the scripts. Beautifully illogical words and images poured out of him all his life. His wife Kathy said: 'Eddie was so serious in what he wrote, but it didn't come out that way.' He worked in a range of genres and shared his angora fetish with at least one character in everything he wrote.

A BBC2 documentary in praise of his life and work, entitled *Look Back in Angora*, concluded that Mr Wood's stream-of-consciousness dialogue was 'like a ransom note pasted together from words randomly cut out of a Korean electronics manual'.

Among his greatest lines are:

'He is as gentle as a kitchen.'

'I guess I have seen everything there is for a policeman to see. Yet I wonder if we ever stop learning. Learning about which we see. Trying to learn more about . . . er . . . (*Pause*) an ounce of prevention.'

'No one wishes to see a man dance.'

'Mistakes are made, but there is no mistake in the thoughts in a man's mind.'

Plastic surgeon: 'Plastic surgery at times seems to me to be (*pause*) very, very complicated.'

'I have but to touch you with my finger and it would mean the end of you all over.'

'This afternoon we had a long telephone conversation earlier in the day.'

'The world is a strange place. All those cars, all going someplace, all carrying humans which are carrying out their lives.'

He was not just skilled in one-liners. He could also do full-blown dialogue:

'This is the twentieth century.'
    'Don't count on it.'

The Worst Film

Voted the worst film ever by the public in the 1978 Golden Turkey awards and the winner of the 1980 New York Worst Film Festival, even after half a century Ed Wood's *Plan 9 from Outer Space* is unrivalled.

Asked to spot flaws in this peerless work, postgraduate film students identified eighty-two. It has everything, including a star who died with just a couple of scenes in the can.

Aliens from a distant galaxy attempt to save Earth's people from themselves by reviving the corpses of an old man in a cape, who looks like Dracula but isn't, his inexplicably glamorous young wife and a police detective who was too heavy to climb out of his own grave. An ex-marine pilot punches the peace-loving leader of the aliens and a flying saucer explodes. That is the plot in a nutshell, but there is so much more to it. The willing suspension of disbelief has never been more comprehensively tested.

To other directors the death of the star actor, Bela Lugosi, would have been an insurmountable obstacle, but Mr Wood was ever inventive. He pulled the masterstroke of replacing him with his wife's chiropractor, who held a cape over his face throughout. Although the chiropractor bore no resemblance to Lugosi whatsoever and was noticeably taller, his wife, Margaret, said 'they both had ears that stuck out'.

Mr Wood wrote the script and then got the First Baptist Church of Beverly Hills to fund it. They agreed on condition that he and his cast were all baptised in a swimming pool while wearing long white robes.

The joy of this superlative production is that it combines an epic storyline with ambitiously threadbare production values. The aliens performed with Brylcreemed hair and Oxford accents while wearing silk pyjamas. The flying saucers were made from a toy kit and dangled with confident authority from yet more visible strings.

☞ 10 ☜

MATTERS OF THE HEART AND SOUL

Meeting One's Spiritual Needs

Our Sort of Cult Leader
The Least Successful Sermon
The Worst Missionary
The Worst Psychic
The Least Successful Quest for Spiritual Perfection
The Least Successful Feng Shui Report
The Worst-Selling Book
The Least Successful Prediction
The Most Inaccurately Addressed Letter

True Romance

The Least Successful Father Christmas
The Least Successful Attempt to Murder a Spouse
The Least Successful Wedding Present
The Most Prolific Divorcees
The Least Successful Romantic Gesture
The Least Successful Suicide Pact
The Greatest Faux Pas
The Least Successful Refereeing

'My imperfections and failures are as much a
blessing from God as my successes.'

MAHATMA GANDHI

Our Sort of Cult Leader

The supreme cult leader is Hon-Ming Chen, who told his followers that God would appear on a Dallas shopping channel at one minute past midnight on 25 March 1998. In this divine broadcast God would announce his intention to descend in person at 10 a.m. the following Tuesday in the garden of Mr Chen's house at 3,513 Ridgedale Avenue in Garland, Texas, where a shrine had been built in readiness from five radial tyres, some plywood and a few lamp posts.

Confident in their prophet, the 150 members of God's Salvation Church, mainly Taiwanese Texans, who wear uniform white cowboy hats, arrived at their leader's house to watch the momentous broadcast. All they got was the snowstorm static which begins as soon as the station closes down.

When God did not appear the following Tuesday either, or walk through walls as promised, a splendidly contrite Mr Chen gave a press conference in which he said his prophecies were nonsense and he advised everyone not to believe anything he said in future. He then offered reporters a ten-minute window of opportunity in which to stone or crucify him.

When no one took him up on this offer, he travelled in a rented minivan to Lake Ontario, where at the end of the world God is to rescue him and his followers in a flying saucer.

In spite of these setbacks, several church members said they were still very committed to Mr Chen's teachings. He also believes that Christ has come back to earth in the form of a six-foot, twenty-eight-year-old Canadian who bears a striking resemblance to Abraham Lincoln and is currently living in Vancouver.

The Least Successful Sermon

Outside it thundered mightily when the Reverend Don Hardman, a travelling evangelist, preached at the First Baptist Church in Forest, Hardin County, Ohio in July 2003. Addressing the congregation on the theme of 'God Speaks in Thunder', he raised his eyes to the heavens, briefly discussed penance and then asked for a sign from God.

Moments later a lightning bolt struck the steeple, blew up the sound system and set the church on fire, causing damage estimated at $20,000. 'He asked for a sign and he got it,' said a member of his flock.

The Worst Missionary

During his thirty years working as a missionary in Africa the explorer David Livingstone only converted one person to Christianity, whom he later excommunicated when his convert fell out with him and left to form his own church.

Converting King Sechele of the BaKwêna tribe was something of a coup, but there were problems. First, he lost his rainmaking abilities as soon as he was baptised, and there was a drought. Then he had second thoughts about giving up all his wives for a monogamous ideal that had never fully grabbed him.

When the King started 'honouring his wives again' there was heady satisfaction among the BaKwêna, but Livingstone became furious and stormed off, never to incite another conversion on his African travels. The King had no sooner been excommunicated than he formed his own church, which combined muscular Christianity with a proper understanding of polygamy and rain-related incantations. The drought ended soon afterwards.

The Worst Psychic

The Amazing Criswell was an American psychic known for his wildly inaccurate predictions. Born Jeron Criswell King, he started modestly enough and in the 1960s predicted that 'an outburst of cannibalism' would terrorise Pittsburgh. Getting into his stride, he foretold that London would be completely wiped out by a meteor on 18 October 1988, that a ray from space would hit Denver, turning metal into rubber and causing horrific accidents at amusement parks, and that the first Interplanetary Congress would take place on 10 March 1990 in the New Convention Centre at Las Vegas with leading citizens present from Mars, Venus, Neptune and the moon. 'Governor Sawyer will make the opening address,' said Criswell, who was only just warming up.

Naturally his predictions were syndicated across America and he was given his own television show, *Criswell Predicts*, on which he appeared flamboyantly dressed with spit-curled hair and a sequinned tuxedo. He also owned a coffin in which he claimed to sleep.

He addressed the audience in a spookily stentorian voice: 'You are interested in the unknown, the mysterious, the unexplainable,' he would say. 'That is why you are here.' Among his more mysterious and unexplainable predictions was one claiming that every woman in a major American city would lose her hair with the result that the whole district would be put under martial law and 'several hairdressers will be murdered'.

His most popular prediction was that the United States of America would in the future be swept by a cloud of aphrodisiac fragrance invented in error by a scientist while researching an improved antiseptic spray. Awash with unbridled passion, America would have to close its borders to stop people trying to get in. 'I predict that many foreign leaders will find excuses to visit the United States on so-called diplomatic missions and their behaviour will be shocking beyond belief.' One Spanish diplomat in particular would be sent home in disgrace.

Off-screen he was the personal psychic of Mae West and predicted that she would become the first female president of the USA, whereupon she, Criswell and George Liberace, brother of the showman pianist, would travel by rocket to the moon.

In his private life he married a former speakeasy dancer called Halo Meadows, whom a neighbour described as 'quite mad'. Mrs Criswell had a huge standard poodle called Buttercup which she was convinced was the reincarnation of her cousin, Thomas.

Asked about his predictions, Criswell replied: 'I am not sure what they mean, but they are all based on subconscious realisations.' He added: 'I am not really an extrovert, just impervious to criticism of any kind.' To this day a company in America sells fridge magnets, thongs and other essential items bearing his ever popular catchphrase: 'I see all.'

The Least Successful Quest for Spiritual Perfection

In August 2006 Jim Nelson decided he was going to become 'a perfect person by fasting'. To this end he gave up his job in the hotel industry and moved to the forest outside Whistler Village, North Vancouver. He had already fasted for thirty days when he decided to try sixty and become even more perfect.

His fast ended on 19 December when he walked into the village, threw a rock through the window of a luxury golf-course condominium, broke in, raided the fridge, pigged out on chilli, cream cheese and tortillas, then ripped open Christmas presents in search of chocolates before slipping into a stupor and passing out on the kitchen floor where the householder found him several hours later surrounded by wrapping paper.

'The inner animal got control of me,' he said.

The Least Successful Feng Shui Report

Just as contracts were due to be exchanged in 1999 on a four-bedroom cottage in East Morton, West Yorkshire, the buyers pulled out after a dreadful feng shui report suggesting that the purchase would bring bad luck. It said the house was not only 'on the line of geopathic stress' but also suffered from 'negative predecessor chi' due to the hard times endured by poor mill workers who had been its earlier inhabitants. Worse still, the stone wall at the front resulted in 'blocked chi' and a power line caused 'bad feng shui which could particularly affect your eldest daughter'.

Instead Andrew Snape and his girlfriend Claire Shuttleworth bought the cottage. Shortly after moving in they won £100 on the lottery, Ms Shuttleworth found a new job, Mr Snape was promoted and then the house appreciated in value by £20,000 overnight. ''We've had a run of really good luck,' said Mr Snape.

The Worst-Selling Book

Sensing a huge public demand, Pavilion Books put together a volume to mark the visit to Britain of Pope John Paul II in 1982. Entitled *The Papal Visit: Official Souvenir*, this book had everything, including a marvellous author who had enjoyed an earlier success with his biography of Percy Thrower, the first TV gardener.

It was lavishly illustrated with smiling nuns, waving children and enough cardinals to sate even the most avid enthusiast. There were four separate pictures of the supreme pontiff kissing airport runways, an aerial view of his address to twenty-five thousand Poles at Crystal Palace and a small photograph of an elderly man from Oldham holding a banner which read: 'I want to touch him.'

With justifiable pride Russell Ash, a director of Pavilion books, said: 'I would like to offer this as the worst-selling book of all time. A hundred thousand copies lumbered round the country with the papal entourage. We sold six.'

The Least Successful Prediction

In 1997 *Old Moore's Almanack* made a startling prediction. Uncannily it forecast that Prince Charles would divorce that year. 'There is movement in his astrological charts which indicates this possibility,' it said.

Prince Charles had in fact, amidst acres of unmissable worldwide media coverage, already divorced a year previously, in 1996. 'It was just an old-fashioned cock-up,' said Barry Belasco, the *Almanack*'s editor. 'Astrology is not a precise art.'

The Most Inaccurately Addressed Letter

The most incorrectly addressed letter ever received came from Uganda for the Reverend Ian Gooding of Stanton-by-Dale in Derbyshire in May 1994. This special document was addressed to 'The Rev Tan Eb-Godding-Same, Stanton-by Dale, Bekesntonica, Mederibys Do 74 Qam, Tel76Keston1/286823/8324884, United Kingdom'.

TRUE ROMANCE

'I honestly think it is better to be a failure at
something you love than to be a success at
something you hate.'

GEORGE BURNS

The Least Successful Father Christmas

In December 1997 a two-year-old boy climbed onto
Father Christmas's lap at a Brooklyn shopping centre and said, 'Santa is Daddy,' whereupon his mother,
who had been looking for Daddy since the summer,
served child-support papers on him in front of some
seriously astonished elves. When Father Christmas
escaped through the toy hall, she came back later,
took him by surprise and jumped on him in the
grotto. Eventually he was forced to take the papers.
'He put them in his sack,' his wife said.

The Least Successful Attempt to Murder
a Spouse

Aided by her boyfriend Donald, Frances Toto made
seven attempts to despatch her husband, Tony,
without him once realising there was a problem. In
the first attempt in 1982 Donald lay in wait with a
.38 revolver, but Tony spoiled everything by arriving from an unexpected direction.

For the second attempt they enlisted a fourteen-year-old boy to tie a tripwire across the steps of Tony's front door and hide in the shrubbery with a baseball bat. Tony fell over the wire, but he assumed it was a practical joke, laughing happily while the boy panicked and fled. Donald next tried to blow up Tony's car. 'That didn't work either,' he said resignedly.

A friend called Anthony was now employed, who hid in the bedroom and shot him. Next morning Tony woke up feeling a bit under the weather and demanding to know what was going on. Frances persuaded her husband that he had flu. She sent him back to bed and gave him chicken soup laced with an overdose of barbiturates.

At this point things got serious. Frances, Donald and Anthony decided to hire two gunmen, called Ronald and Donald. Following a prearranged plan, this second Donald lurked outside the bedroom with yet another baseball bat while Ronald walked in and shot Tony in the chest. They had returned to the sitting room and were discussing payment with Frances when Tony walked in and asked if he could speak to his wife in private. Various things were beginning to worry him.

Frances reassured him and reiterated that his flu was really shocking. Making the seventh and final attempt, she fed him more chicken soup and barbiturates, without realising that the drug retards internal bleeding and was thus keeping Tony alive.

Overhearing Ronald and the second Donald discussing their afternoon's work in a bar, two policemen raced round in a squad car to see Tony, who refused to believe it when told he had been shot.

'We still love each other,' said Tony, who was happily reunited with Frances when she was released from prison. 'I don't understand why people break up over silly things.'

The Least Successful Wedding Present

Wishing to impress his new bride, Peter Gillings of Mellis in Suffolk decided to give her the ultimate wedding present: the things that mattered most to him in the whole world after her.

In March 1994, barely able to contain his excitement, he gave her a bomber cockpit, a Jaguar jet nose cone, a Flying Fortress wheel, bomb casings, two dud Sidewinder missiles and a selection of priceless old wing parts. Showing that there was no limit to either his love or his generosity, he also threw in a ten-foot model of a Trident warhead, several old military uniforms, swords, daggers, bayonets, helmets, rifles and a select range of handguns from his own beloved personal collection, which had taken a lifetime to gather.

This man is one of the last great romantics and his wife's response was, quite frankly, astonishing.

Instead of being utterly thrilled by these fabulous gifts, Mrs Gillings asked for a divorce. 'I was furious,' she said later. 'I only have a small flat and I don't want it turned into a scrap yard. Either that junk goes or I do.'

The Most Prolific Divorcees

In the western world Glynn 'Scotty' Wolfe has no rivals. A Baptist minister and former marriage counsellor, he was divorced twenty-eight times. 'Everyone should get married. I always have been,' said Mr Wolfe, who only had twenty-six mothers-in-law because he married two of his wives twice.

He divorced wife number twenty-three on the grounds that she used his toothbrush and number twenty-six because she ate sunflower seeds in bed.

In 1996 Mr Wolfe, who always kept a couple of wedding dresses in his wardrobe in readiness, was married for the twenty-ninth and last time to Linda Essex, the world's most divorced woman. She had been divorced only twenty-six times, which is testimony to the more monogamous nature of women.

Known in her time as Mrs Scott, Mrs Street, Mrs Smith, Mrs Moyer, Mrs Massey, Mrs McMillan, Mrs Beresford, Mrs Chandler, Mrs Essex, Mrs Gourlay, Mrs Chadwick and Mrs Stutzman among others, she was born Linda Lou Taylor and came from Anderson, Indiana, which boasts the largest ball of dried paint in the world. In her neighbourhood, she said, 'all the boys wanted to marry me'. By 1998 most of them had.

She received 121 proposals of marriage so had to be very selective. Among her husbands were two gay men and a one-eyed convict. She married one husband three times and another for only three days. 'In some of these towns where world record-holders live they have signs outside the city limits,' Mrs Wolfe once said. 'I wouldn't mind if Anderson would have a sign like that.'

By the time she became the final Mrs Wolfe she was living in a retirement complex and 'praying all day'. Cynics said they only got married for a TV documentary, but Mrs Wolfe said: 'As soon as I saw him, I knew I cared for him.'

The Least Successful Romantic Gesture

Wishing to impress his girlfriend, Leslie Pook, and perhaps influenced by the balcony scene in *Romeo and Juliet*, Stephen O'Halloran arrived at her home in Fleetwood in March 1990 under cover of darkness. Armed with a clothes-line prop and clutching a bargain bucket of Kentucky Fried Chicken, he attempted to pole-vault through her bedroom window as she slept.

Propelling himself at speed towards Miss Pook's chamber, his pole snapped and Mr O'Halloran flew into the wall. The dull, mellifluous thud did not awaken his sleeping paramour, but it did arouse her neighbour, who called the police. On arrival they found Mr O'Halloran wandering in a dazed state around the garden.

Challenged as to the legality, wisdom and Health and Safety aspects of his endeavour, Miss Pook's thwarted admirer became disputatious. Arrested at the scene, he was led away. Miss Pook remained asleep throughout.

The Least Successful Suicide Pact

Two Polish seventeen-year-olds, Beata and Kamil, wanted to marry but their parents forbade it. Also inspired by the example of Romeo and Juliet, they went to a chemist and asked for 'the strongest poison in the shop'.

Smelling a rat, the chemist gave them a bottle of laxative instead. Clutching the potion that would seal their union in eternity, they booked into a hotel. Having requested an economy room without a bathroom or toilet, they locked the door, threw the key out of the window, swallowed the entire bottle of their potion and lay entwined on the bed to expire in each other's arms.

It was some while before they dared to call room service. 'The room had to be fumigated,' said the hotel manager. 'When they came out the couple said they now found each other disgusting and the engagement was off.'

The Greatest Faux Pas

Officially listed as the greatest engagement faux pas in *The Guinness Book of Records*, this event is still remembered 135 years later and ensured that the name of 'Gordon Bennett' passed into the English language.

Son of the *New York Herald*'s founder, James Gordon Bennett became engaged in 1876 to the wealthy socialite Caroline May. The *Edwardsville Intelligencer* reported on the opulent preparations right down to Miss May's $20,000 trousseau which arrived from Europe.

It was therefore of great interest to many when Mr Bennett arrived substantially inebriated at a New Year's party held by his fiancée's father. In full view of his fiancée, her father and all the guests, our hero urinated in the fireplace, mistaking it for the lavatory. Some reports say it was the grand piano, as if that mattered.

Local papers reported next morning that the engagement was off. Perhaps surprisingly, Mr Bennett fled to Melton Mowbray, which may or may not have made things better.

Given our advanced modern standards, it is extraordinary that any one of us has not broken this record long ago.

The Least Successful Refereeing

Phil Pawsey made his unique contribution to football refereeing at the match between Northleach Town and Smith's Athletic in the Endsleigh Cheltenham League first division in January 1998.

The match was like any other until Mr Pawsey's wife, Trish, ran onto the pitch demanding his door keys because she had locked herself out. He halted the game so he could find them.

This took so long that by the time he returned it was too dark to play the remaining six minutes. He had no choice but to abandon the game.

❧ 11 ☙

WORKING WITH ANIMALS

The Least Successful Attempt to Talk to Animals
The Least Successful Sheepdog
The Least Successful Rat Repellent
The Least Successful Discovery of a New Species
The Worst Grand National
Devon Loch: A Tribute
The Worst Jockey
The Least Successful Hospital Visit
The Worst Bear Rescue
The Least Successful Attempt to Slaughter a Pig
The Longest Cow Round-Up

'Good people are good because they have come to wisdom through failure.'

WILLIAM SAROYAN

The Least Successful Attempt to Talk to Animals

In a pioneering advance for inter-species communication, two neighbours in south Devon hooted at one another for a year, each thinking the other was an owl.

A keen ornithologist, Neil Simmons had been studying the calls of tawny owls in an oak tree at the bottom of his garden when he decided to attempt conversation with his own periodic hootings. It was not until 1996, when Fred Cornes moved in next door, that his persistence finally paid off.

Success was instant.

Nightly for twelve months they both crept into the garden and every single one of their calls was met with an instant and gratifying reply.

They would still be doing this pioneering work but for a chance conversation in which Mrs Simmons told Mrs Cornes how excited her husband got when the owl hooted back. 'He logs each call and is trying to modify his to-whit to-whoo to mimic the other owl,' she explained. 'That's funny . . .' said Mrs Cornes and the research project came to an end.

The Least Successful Sheepdog

In 1986 Mandi Brooker of Johannesburg decided there was no reason why only country people should take part in sheepdog trials. Striking a blow for townies everywhere, she acquired a Border collie called Cindy and trained it in her suburban home and garden.

Entering a trial at rural Pietermaritzburg, this splendid dog herded a flock of sheep past the finishing pen, out of the field, across the grounds of a boarding school, up two flights of stairs and into the girls' dormitory. That evening at a celebration dinner the deputy headmaster sat next to our shepherd. 'Will you', he asked, pausing hesitantly, 'be competing again tomorrow?'

Even so this is not the least successful sheepdog trial on record. In July 1991 at the fortieth annual show of the Lanchester Agricultural Society a sheepdog was chased from the field by a flock of sheep.

The Least Successful Rat Repellent

Keen to be at the forefront of rodent control, Rentokil decided in the 1990s to test the very latest state-of-the-art technology, an ultrasonic device that promised to drive rats away by sound alone. Completely surpassing all expectations, the rats not only ate their food regardless, but also gnawed through the plastic casing and destroyed the go-ahead contraption. The firm manufacturing it decided to employ Rentokil to protect their ultrasonic gadgets from rats using conventional means.

The Least Successful Discovery of a New Species

Amidst feverish international excitement a new species of mammal was discovered in an isolated area of Vietnam in 1995. Known as a tuoa, this small deer-like breed from the same family as the ox was hailed by the Vietnamese branch of the World Wildlife Fund as 'the biological equivalent of discovering a new planet'.

The animal was found in December. In January it was eaten by villagers.

The Worst Grand National

The greatest ever Grand National got off to a textbook false start in 1996 when the horses jumped the flag and had to be called back before the first fence. However, this was just an aperitif before a sumptuous banquet. The second attempt was a far superior false start. When the official called them back again, his flag failed to unfurl, with historic consequences.

[201]

Of the thirty-nine runners thirty went on to complete the entire Grand National course while everyone at Aintree did their best to stop them. The crowd roared. Trainers gesticulated. When officials waved red flags, the jockeys thought they were animal rights protestors who had invaded the course earlier. In a brave last-ditch attempt to halt the race a solitary cone was placed in front of a jump. Nine horses completed the course before the race was abandoned. Esha Ness won in the second fastest time ever.

The whole marvellous event was televised live to viewers worldwide. Watching on a giant screen at the Happy Valley Racecourse in Hong Kong, a breathless Katy Chiu said: 'The Chinese understand nothing of this: horses jumping fences. You tell me this is not a race and I tell you this is the most exciting race we have ever seen.'

Devon Loch: A Tribute

Owned by the Queen Mother, Devon Loch was one of the most distinguished horses ever to grace British racing. In the 1956 Grand National he became the most famous example on record of an animal snatching defeat from the jaws of victory. This prestigious charger was galloping towards the finishing line five lengths ahead of the field and in grave danger of not only breaking the record for the fastest ever Grand National win, but also becoming the first victorious royal horse in fifty-six years.

Something had to be done. With forty yards to go, in front of the royal box and before the Queen Mother herself, this imaginative horse executed the most exquisite leap. Full of joy and hopeful yearning, his legs outstretched like a gazelle in flight, he floated momentarily like gossamer in a spring breeze before he plunged to the ground in the most perfect collapse and failed to finish the course. Reuters said he had 'belly flopped', which shows just how little poetry there is in a news agency.

The Worst Jockey

The most important British jockey, Anthony Knott took up horse racing in 1980 at the age of sixteen and did not win his first race until twenty-eight years later, when he was forty-four. His previous best results were two fifth-place finishes. 'I used to sit and watch the Seabiscuit film. It kept me going.'

Mr Knott always claimed that he 'had one race' in him. This is a reference to the regrettable occasion when he won the 2.30 at Wincanton on 20 November 2008, riding Wise Men Say. To his great credit he did everything possible to lose this race as well. He stood up on his irons and started celebrating before he crossed the line so that he was almost overtaken in the final furlong.

He retired immediately, but rejected the suggestion that he had quit while he was ahead. 'I'm not ahead,' he pointed out. 'I've never been ahead.'

The Least Successful Hospital Visit

In June 2010 Mrs Connie Everett of Kitimat, British Columbia, was taken to hospital after colliding with a moose while driving to visit her sister, Mrs Yvonne Studley, who was in hospital after colliding with a moose.

The Worst Bear Rescue

In February 1991 a crowd of around fifty people formed in Keithville, Louisiana, to watch a vet and a game warden armed with tranquillising darts rescue a black bear that was stuck high up in a pine tree. Many brought their own sandwiches to make a night of it. Extra police were called in. Several wildlife refuges were alerted to receive the animal. As night fell spotlights and nets were strung between the trees to catch it.

At first the animal was quite active, but the stungun darts seem to calm it down briefly. To the gasps and dismay of onlookers, the bear then panicked and began flapping wildly. After eight hours there was only one option. They had to cut the tree down. Shortly before sunrise the crowd watched as the team rescued a heavily sedated black dustbin liner.

The Least Successful Attempt to
Slaughter a Pig

In January 1998 Arnoldo Dijulio, a council road-sweeper, delivered two Tamworth pigs that he had reared in his back garden to a slaughterhouse in Malmesbury, Wiltshire. His idea was to sell the pigs for £50 as hand-reared pork.

The pigs' idea was that they would burrow under the perimeter fence, dash over the road, swim across the River Avon and lie low while they became national heroes, inflaming animal lovers, militant vegetarians and the world's press in a battle to save them from slaughter.

Mr Dijulio told the abattoir he would be right back with the pigs and spent the next eight days hunting for them without success. As news of this escape spread their celebrity status grew. After three days the pigs were being trailed by a small army of animal handlers, RSPCA officers, abattoir staff, police, tracker dogs and Fleet Street reporters, and were now known as Butch and Sundance. A tempting Tamworth sow was also flaunted as bait.

From time to time, the pigs would emerge from the undergrowth briefly, toy with their hunters and disappear again. On the fourth day Sundance was spotted in the back garden of a local resident. Police managed to corner this noble beast, while Mr Dijulio attempted a capture. Sundance escaped into the undergrowth.

The whereabouts of Butch was unknown, although a local clairvoyant rang the police daily to say he knew where she was.

A full week after the great escape Butch was captured by a crack rescue team of *Daily Mail* reporters and taken to a secret location away from rival newspapers and media organisations.

Sundance, who was probably the ringleader, had another thirty-six hours of freedom while reporters, photographers, vets, police and Mr Dijulio scoured the countryside.

Next morning, police and an RSPCA officer – watched by a crowd of sixty – chased her for two hours before giving up. The following day it took eight men, two dogs and three tranquilliser darts in a twenty-four-hour operation to get Sundance under lock and key at a vet's surgery. The vet, Francis Baird, eventually padlocked the doors and chained them together. 'I would describe these pigs as extremely cunning and devious,' said PC Roger Bull.

Scores of reporters witnessed this dramatic end. An American journalist, Donatella Lorch, spoke for all the foreign correspondents when she said: 'We all went wild at the sight of journalists doing very serious stand-up reports about the pigs in the middle of a field.'

One British firm made soft-toy versions of 'The Tamworth Two', as they became known. A pigs-on-the-run movie was also made of their exploits, but it was highly sensationalised and showed them trying to reach their spiritual home in Tamworth pursued by an evil slaughterhouse manager.

Faced with worldwide opposition to his slaughter plans, Mr Dijulio decided to sell the pigs to the *Daily Mail*. 'I am surprised by the interest,' he said. The *Mail* has so far paid for twelve years of comfortable retirement. At the advanced age of thirteen Butch was eventually cremated. Sundance is now fourteen and still going strong at the Ashford Rare Breeds Farm in Kent.

The Longest Cow Round-Up

In the longest round-up in the history of the man–cow interface Cree Mackenzie took two years to get just nine cows into the same pen. It began in 1992 when he put his cattle out to graze on Little Bernera, a tiny island off the Isle of Lewis in the Outer Hebrides.

It was the perfect arrangement for Mr Mackenzie and a complete blast for the cows, but then he bought a new rogue bullock who was a troublemaker. 'He was from Oban,' said Mr Mackenzie, which explained everything. 'He was not local and did not have the same manners.' In no time the whole herd had gone feral. 'He caused an insurrection. They all went wild and would not do as they were told.'

One day he decided to round them up for the cattle market. No cow in its right mind is going to agree to this so they went berserk, smashing through six-foot fences and hoofing it.

First, Mr Mackenzie employed twenty-four cattlemen to round them up, but the cows were having none of it. 'They chased them round the island and the cattle outwitted them by swimming out into the loch where they could not be reached.' Fed up after several months chasing recalcitrant heifers round the Outer Hebrides, Mr Mackenzie appealed for volunteers to camp on the island and gain the cows' confidence. No one was attracted by this scheme.

In 1993, sensing a challenge, the army offered to help. 'They made a stockade with a rope attached to the gate and watched through binoculars. The cows wrecked it and the stockade had to be rebuilt.' After two years they finally coaxed one cow into this contraption with food.

Seeing that the game was up and it was best not to mess with the military, the other eight cows swam across the water and surrendered.

'It's been a long hard slog,' said Mr Mackenzie, 'but at least I didn't have to feed them for two years.'

☞ 12 ☜

THIS SPORTING LIFE

Boat Race Sinkings: Latest
News from the Back of the Grid
The Least Exciting Race
The Most Boxing Defeats
The Worst Golfer
The Worst Knockout
The Longest Cricket Match without a Run
The Worst Heavyweight Title Fight
The Worst Rugby Tour Match
The Least Successful Victory Celebration
The Worst Fielding
The Least Successful Rugby Match
The Worst Olympic Swimming Heat
The Worst Batsmen
The Worst Olympic Bobsleigh Race
The Worst Olympic Discus Thrower
The Worst Olympic Cross-Country Skiing

The Beautiful Game

The Worst World Cup Match
The Fastest Sacking of a Football Manager
The Worst Premiership Footballer

Quiz

The Worst Football Team in Britain

*

'There are some defeats that are more triumphant
than victories.'
MICHEL DE MONTAIGNE

Boat Race Sinkings: Latest

It had been eighty-five long, weary years since both crews sank in the electrifying Oxford and Cambridge boat race of 1912. Many were giving up hope that it would ever happen again. Year after year Oxford and Cambridge had been coursing predictably up and down the River Thames, still very much afloat. Then in 1997 they were invited to race a crew from Brazil at the first ever international regatta held on a tributary of the Amazon.

Showing that we have much to learn from this vibrant culture, the Oxbridge crews were hot-footing it down the Rio Negro when a flotilla of pleasantly unruly spectators sailed into the rowing lanes to get a better view. Ignoring urgent loudspeaker alerts, several speedboats at full throttle created the perfect conditions, swerving in and out of the crews' path.

'We were hit by one large wave. It was all over in a flash,' said Charlie Humphreys, a distinguished member of the historic Oxford crew which shook off the eighty-five-year jinx and went down first. Cambridge sank minutes later. Understandably, the Brazilian spectators, who had never seen a British boat race before, decided that this was fabulous entertainment and the event must be repeated as soon as possible. Afterwards the Oxford and Cambridge crews danced a celebratory samba, as you would expect.

News from the Back of the Grid

While others are absorbed by the leaders in a Formula One race, our eyes are naturally trained at the other end where genius reigns, records abound and the competition is really fierce.

Marco Apicella had the shortest Formula One racing career in history, competing in just one race. He almost made it to the first corner in the Italian Grand Prix of 1993 before hurtling off the track after only eight hundred metres and deciding not to enter again. It lasted seconds.

Meanwhile, Al Pease is the only Formula One driver ever to be disqualified for being too slow. He entered three Canadian Grand Prix of which the most spectacular was in 1967. Here he finished forty-three laps behind the winner, which is half the race, travelling at an average speed of 44 mph.

He was delayed for six laps at the beginning when his car would not start. After a few laps the engine stalled and then the battery went flat, so he ran all the way up the very hilly circuit to the pits to get a new battery. He then ran all the way back and fitted it himself.

For sheer inventiveness in the crash department Taki Inoue leads the field. Impressively, his car rolled upside down in 1995 while he was being towed back to the pit. He was later run over by the fire marshal arriving to extinguish his smoking vehicle.

Spending as much time off the track as on it during a race, he was on top form in the final Australian Grand Prix of that year. He spun into a wall while watching Schumacher in his mirror as he was about to be lapped. Asked to assess his career in Formula One by *F1 Racing* magazine, he replied: 'Smoke too much, drink too much, lazy bastard.'

The Least Exciting Race

Nothing was too much trouble in the preparations for the community fun run at the Waterlooville Festival in Hampshire in September 1994. A special registration desk was set up to process all the entries and 150 shirt numbers had been printed in readiness for the event. Volunteer timekeepers had stopwatches at the ready. The mile-long course round a recreation ground was marked out with paint and supervised by six race marshals. A St John Ambulance crew was on standby in case of emergencies. Dozens of medals were laid out for the presentation ceremony.

A large crowd had formed to line the course and excitement had reached fever pitch when it turned out that only one person had entered the race, a seven-year-old boy called Michael Biddell, who arrived in his school PE kit.

Enthralled by this spectacle, the crowd roared, cheered and were ecstatic with pleasure as this splendid boy sprinted into the lead and, straining every muscle and sinew, came first or, to look on the bright side, last. 'The medals did not have 1994 on them so we can use them again next year,' a member of the organising committee said.

The Most Boxing Defeats

One of the top boxers in our field is the immortal Peter Buckley, who fought three hundred noble bouts in his career and lost a magnificent 256 of them. He often turned up for a fight with black eyes from a previous encounter.

Writing appreciatively in the *Sunday Times* in 2008, Ron Lewis said that Buckley had matured into a consistent loser. 'He has kept himself in a constant state of readiness, ready to lose a fight at a moment's notice anywhere in the country.' In his career he lost to forty-two future world, European, Commonwealth and British champions.

'I get a call a couple of hours before a fight. I usually say yes. If you phone up a bricklayer and ask him to build a wall, he doesn't ask for three weeks to prepare,' said Buckley, who once famously accepted a bout at 8 p.m. on the night of the fight.

'Boxing has been good to me,' he said on his retirement from the ring. 'But I definitely won't miss getting punched in the face for a living.'

The only person with a better record is the great American pugilist Reggie Strickland who lost 276 fights in his career, which is more than any other boxer. He also undertook more fights than anyone else (363) because he was understandably in great demand as an opponent.

The Worst Golfer

The immortal Maurice Flitcroft became the world's worst golfer in 1976 when he entered the British Open Championships never having played a full round of golf in his life. Arriving with a set of cheap mail-order golf clubs, he took 121 strokes to complete the course, which is the worst ever score in the Open's history. As a result the great man was banned from every golf club in the country.

Encouraged by this, he decided to turn professional, but it was difficult to find anywhere that would allow him to practise. Turned away from Barrow Golf Club as a result of several clothing code infringements, often relating to his bobble hat, he got up at 4 a.m. to practise on their course in the dark while the members were asleep.

Believing that he would one day win the Open, Mr Flitcroft continued to enter this contest annually under a range of pseudonyms: Gerald Hoppy, James Dean Jolly, Arnold Palm Tree and Count Manfred von Hoffmanstal. He also adopted a range of disguises, not least a large handlebar moustache dyed with vegetable colouring and a deerstalker hat. On each occasion he was chased off the course by the organisers after a succession of awe-inspiring shots revealed his true identity. Once they even employed a handwriting expert to detect his fake entry application.

In 1988 the Blythfield Country Club in Grand Rapids, Michigan, initiated the Maurice Flitcroft Member-Guest Tournament. Mr Flitcroft himself was flown over to play in this event. On arrival he told members of the club that it was the first time he and his wife had been out of the house together since their gas oven exploded.

By the time of the twenty-second Flitcroft Tournament in May 2000, this admirable club featured a golf green with an encouraging twelve-inch-wide hole.

The Worst Knockout

At the 1982 North American Championships in Las Vegas the Cuban heavyweight Pedro Cardenas showed how important the element of surprise is in a contact sport. Fighting the Canadian boxer Willie DeWitt, he ducked, bobbed, weaved, swung a left hook, missed his opponent and knocked out the referee, Bert Lowes.

The first round continued with a replacement referee, who had the advantage of being much smaller than Mr Lowes and therefore out of punching range. Great boxers are versatile, however, and Cardenas ducked, bobbed, weaved and with a repeat left hook struck a glancing blow that slid downwards and knocked out the second referee. With our man in such imperious form the bout was delayed due to a general unwillingness to take over as ref.

His night's work done, the great Cuban was himself knocked out in the second round.

The Longest Cricket Match without a Run

We still await the perfect cricket game in which neither side scores a run at all, but until then we must make do with the glorious match in July 2004 between Goldsborough and Dishforth in the Nidderdale and District League.

Batting first, Goldsborough showed Dishforth a thing or two when the whole team was bowled out for 0. The other team's captain marvelled at their performance: 'Everything they hit just went wrong.'

Goldsborough had kept their half of the bargain and now it was Dishforth's turn to bat. Excitement grew to fever pitch as their first two batsmen were both out before they could score a run. Was perfection imminent?

Sadly, there followed a complete collapse and Dan Bettles Hall, who will have to live with the memory of this forever, scored a run.

'It beats shopping on Saturday,' said the Goldsborough captain.

The Worst Heavyweight Title Fight

During the world heavyweight title bout against Lennox Lewis in 1997, Oliver McCall burst into tears and refused to throw a punch, which was a pleasingly sensible reaction. It is frankly amazing that this has not happened before.

Entering into the spirit of things, Lewis stopped punching as well and the result was a very lovely fifth round with no one hitting anyone at all. Incredibly, Mr McCall was disqualified. A psychiatrist who examined this ultimate pugilist for ninety minutes after the fight said: 'I think his mental state is just fine.'

The TV commentators were also on top form. Minutes before our boxer burst into tears one of them said: 'I tell you what, this fellow McCall is in good shape.' His colleague replied: 'I really feel this fight could go all the way.'

The Worst Rugby Tour Match

Thanks to an administrative error during their Romanian tour in May 2000, the Dorchester Gladiators, an over-forties veteran rugby team, ran out to find that they were playing Romania's top club, Steaua Bucharest, which included nine internationals. They also discovered the match was being broadcast live on national television and played in front of thousands of spectators, who had been led to believe the Gladiators were a top British team.

'It frightened us to death at first,' said the Gladiators' full-back, Dave Seddon, who was one of the younger players at forty-five. 'We had been out for a few beers the night before and were all feeling a bit fragile. We are no longer at our peak.'

Nigel Jones, a forty-three-year-old surveyor, said: 'We started to get worried when our hosts asked us if we wanted to do a training session the night before, which is not exactly our style. We did our pre-match build-up in the bar and didn't get in until 4 a.m. The match began at eleven.'

When they saw that their opponents were fit athletes in their twenties, the Gladiators tried to convince them that they were seriously awful, but the Romanians assumed this was mind games. 'They refused to believe us,' said Mr Jones. 'They started warming up like real professionals and we just stood about smoking a few cigarettes knowing we were in real trouble.'

The match ended 61–17 after the Romanians eased off when they realised they were in no danger of losing. The highlights were shown on the TV news.

The Least Successful Victory Celebration

In one of the great moments of horse-racing history the Irish jockey Roger Loughran showed the importance of holding something in reserve for the final push. Riding Central House in the Paddy Power Dial a Bet Chase at Leopardstown in 2005, he was in the lead after two miles and the finishing line was a hundred yards away.

The situation looked very serious indeed, but with victory staring him in the face, he still had something up his sleeve and mistook an upright bundle of birch for the finishing line. He stood up on his stirrups, punched the air in victory, waved, smiled and was just saluting the crowd with his whip when he was overtaken by Hi Cloy and Fota Island, lost the race and came third. 'These things happen,' said the horse's trainer.

The Worst Fielding

Although he had played county cricket for Gloucestershire, G. E. Hemingway's greatest achievement came towards the end of the nineteenth century when playing a single-wicket match against his brothers.

He helped to make possible the second worst fielding in any cricket game anywhere. He hit the ball into a bed of nettles, whereupon the fieldsmen quarrelled as to who should recover it. During the argument the batsmen scored 250 runs.

The worst ever fielding was achieved in Western Australia. It happened in 1894 when a batsman named Cogg hit the ball into a tree. The umpire ruled that since the ball remained in view and had not touched the ground, it was still in play. The batsmen started running. The fielders tried climbing the tree to get the ball, but the lower branches broke and they crashed to the ground. The batsmen kept running. An axe was called for but a search proved futile. Eventually one of the fielders arrived with a gun, which was then used to blast away at the tree. By this point the batsmen, now completely exhausted, had stopped running. They had scored 286 runs.

The Least Successful Rugby Match

In June 2006, seventy Russian police officers raced to an amateur rugby match on the outskirts of Rostov and arrested both teams, the referee and all the spectators. Tipped off about a mass brawl between gangs of rival hooligans, they saw nothing to persuade them otherwise.

Match organisers repeatedly explained that this was a game and played for pleasure in much of western Europe and beyond. Understandably the officers found this difficult to believe and locked them up in Rostov police station, where around a hundred rugby enthusiasts spent several hours explaining the rules. They were only released on the strict understanding that they would give written or verbal notification in future before attempting to play this game again.

The Worst Olympic Swimming Heat

The Olympic Games have offered no finer sight than Eric Moussambani, who in the Sydney Olympics entered the 100m freestyle heats even though he had only taken up swimming the previous January. He represented Equatorial Guinea, where he trained in shark- and crocodile-infested waters because the only pool was too full of tourists.

On that memorable day in September 2000 he had already told his coach that he thought a hundred metres was too far, but his coach insisted. There were only two other competitors in his heat and they both fell into the pool before the starting whistle and were disqualified. As a result Eric was in with at least a chance of coming first.

In stark contrast to the futuristic go-faster swimming kit of other Olympians Eric wore traditional swimming trunks with a drawstring untied and visibly dangling. In the first length he did not once put his head under water and then he bravely attempted a tumble turn.

Sensing that they were in the presence of true greatness, the crowd erupted in deafening cheers as he appeared to sink beneath the water during his second and final length. Lifeguards stood poised to rescue him as his stroke shortened and his legs sank. Inspired by a thunderous ovation, he made it to the end. 'I want to send hugs and kisses to the crowd because it was their cheering that kept me going.'

Reflecting on his unique performance, he said: 'What happened to me was worth more than gold. I'm going to jump and dance all night long in celebration of my personal triumph.'

When he returned to the athletes' village a sign had been erected on his door, saying: 'Home of Eric the swimmer'.

The Worst Batsmen

Cricket is a wonderfully restful game apart from the incessant sound of bat on ball and people running up and down, backwards and forwards, all day long until darkness prevents them. Only three batsmen have been a cut above the rest.

John Howarth of Nottinghamshire holds the record for batting in the most first-class matches without scoring a run. He took nineteen wickets as a bowler, but nobody cares about that. In thirteen matches for Nottinghamshire he failed to get a run in seven innings. In retirement he contacted a statistics website to ask who held the record and was told, 'You do.'

For complicated cricket reasons that we cannot possibly be expected to understand, Seymour Clark holds the record for the most innings without scoring a run (nine innings in five matches).

'He was a brilliant wicket-keeper, but no one remembers that,' observed *Wisden Cricket Monthly* of this 1930s Somerset player. 'Everyone remembers his batting.' He bought a new bat when picked for his county, but rarely touched the ball with it.

Even opposing teams tried to help him. Peter Smith, the good-natured Essex spin bowler, did his best to give Mr Clark a chance of scoring a run. In the match against Somerset he deliberately pitched a very gentle ball that bounced twice before reaching the great batsman. 'I couldn't resist it,' he recalled afterwards, 'and I tried to give it an almighty clout.' He missed and was bowled out.

Courtney Walsh is also of lasting importance, having scored an illustrious forty-three ducks in Test matches for the West Indies. In between he averaged eight runs a game, which takes the shine off things.

The Worst Olympic Bobsleigh Race

At the 1988 Winter Olympics the world looked on in awed admiration as Jamaica entered its first ever bobsleigh team despite having no snow, no bobsleighs and, most importantly, no one who had the faintest idea how to do it. American TV channels cleared the airwaves to provide comprehensive coverage of this important event.

They had been urged to enter by two American visitors, who reckoned that if Jamaicans could take part in a pushcart derby and hurtle round Kingston at 60 mph in food vending carts then bobsleighing would be a piece of cake.

Their best hope was to advertise for sprinters who could at least push the sleigh to a fast start and then jump on. When no one even applied for the post, they enlisted four army sprinters, of whom one was Lieutenant Devon Harris. 'Needless to say, I thought it was the most ridiculous idea ever conceived by man,' he said.

Also in the team were Captain Dudley Stokes, the reggae singer Freddie Powell, who was apparently included for his PR value, and Dudley's brother Chris, who was enlisted at the last moment and had less than a week's training before the Olympics.

Even then they had to borrow spare bobsleighs from other countries to compete.

'After blasting off the top of the hill with the seventh fastest start time we crashed in a spectacular fashion only in a way that Jamaicans could,' said Lieutenant Harris, with justifiable national pride.

After their crash they got out and walked across the finishing line with their sleigh to thunderous applause and the admiration of a watching world. They brought bobsleigh racing to an international prominence that more experienced competitors have never managed to equal.

The Worst Olympic Discus Thrower

In the Athens games of 1896 George Stewart Robertson set the world record for the worst throw in Olympic history. At the closing ceremony he recited an ode to athletic prowess which he had composed himself in ancient Greek. 'Greek classics were my proper academic field, so I could hardly resist a go at the Olympics, could I?' he said.

His record worst throw is twenty-five metres, which still seems an awfully long way. It is astonishing that with all the advantages of modern diet and motivational psychology the young athlete of today has not slashed this.

The Worst Olympic Cross-Country Skiing

Philip Boit was a successful middle-distance runner facing a terrible vista of unending triumph which would obviously not hold his interest for long. Needing a challenge in 1996, he started cross-country skiing in his native Kenya, which lacks widespread access to snow.

With no previous experience, this fine athlete gained worldwide coverage and acclaim when he came an unbeatable ninety-second in the 10km cross-country ski race at the 1998 Winter Olympics. The medal ceremony was delayed for Boit to finish because the winner, Bjørn Dæhlie, wanted to hug him. This moved our skier so much that he named one of his sons 'Dæhlie Boit'.

'I was not disappointed,' he said. 'Although I was last, Bjørn Dæhlie commended my effort.'

The greatest ever cross-country skier, however, was the Mexican Roberto Alvarez. At the Calgary Winter Olympics in 1988 he competed in the 50km event although he had never skied further than twenty kilometres before. He came a definitive last in sixty-first place, almost an hour behind the sixtieth-place finisher. He took so long that race organisers sent out a search party.

THE BEAUTIFUL GAME

The Worst World Cup Match

The most rewarding game in the history of the World Cup was a vital qualifying match between Scotland and Estonia on 9 October 1996. Only one team turned up to play because the Estonians were having their lunch, which was completely understandable. Lunch is a very important institution. Who among us does not appreciate the importance of lunch?

Inexplicably, Scotland had complained about the hugely atmospheric floodlighting, which had been borrowed temporarily from Finland. Whole swathes of pitch were shrouded in a most attractive gloom. It was a thrilling chiaroscuro landscape with contrasting light and dark patches in which players could disappear, particularly when taking corners, and, not unlike the ghost of Hamlet's father, suddenly reappear to everybody's surprise.

FIFA changed the kick-off from 6.45 to 3 p.m. after the Scotland manager had complained that the goalkeepers would not be able to see any ball coming in from the left side of the pitch, a technicality that did not persuade the Estonians. They said that they would be arriving for 6.45 as originally planned because it was too late to change the arrangements and the potatoes were already on.

At three o'clock the referee blew his whistle and the Tartan Army of a thousand travelling Scottish fans shouted, 'Get intae them.' Billy Dodds had just kicked off, passing the ball to John Collins, when the referee blew his whistle again after three seconds, ending a game that promised so much free-flowing football. The score was o–o. Obviously it would have been even better if Scotland had lost.

On 11 February 1997 the match was replayed and the score was o–o again, which showed that the presence of a second team was not actually necessary.

The Fastest Sacking of a Football Manager

The record for the fastest sacking of a football manager is held by Torquay United, which fired Leroy Rosenior ten minutes after announcing his appointment. In a report headlined 'Stability is the Key' the local newspaper said the new boss was 'hugely upbeat' at the press conference held to unveil him in May 2007.

Flanked by the chairman and managing director, he said: 'I'm absolutely delighted and really enthused. We want to bring stability to the club first and foremost.'

Ten minutes later Mr Rosenior learned that the club had been taken over during the press conference and the new owners would bring in their own staff.

Committed to excellence, Torquay also hold the record for the fastest own goal in league football. In January 1977 their brilliant centre half Pat Kruse leapt above his own defence and with lightning reactions headed the ball into his own net after only six seconds.

The Worst Premiership Footballer

On 23 November 1996 fans of Southampton Football Club were lucky enough to see Ali Dia in his full glory. By universal acclaim he is the worst footballer ever to play in the premiership.

In the match against Leeds United he came on as a substitute in the thirty-second minute and was himself replaced in the seventy-fifth minute. According to his Southampton teammate Matt Le Tissier, 'he ran round the pitch like Bambi on ice', which gives you some idea how very appealing it must have been. In those unrepeatable minutes he displayed superbly inept ball control that has been described as 'staggeringly below premiership standard'. He went straight into action and missed a stunning open goal from twelve yards as soon as he came on.

He was snapped up by Southampton in the mistaken belief that he had played for the crack French side Paris St Germain and for the Senegal national team, scoring twice in recent weeks. It later emerged that he had, in fact, played once as a substitute for Blyth Spartans, a non-league team, who let him go.

The Least Successful Friendship Cup

In one of the worst-behaved football matches on record Boca Juniors of Argentina lost 3–1 to the Chilean champions Colo Colo on 2 May 1991. Against a background of crowd taunts and personal insults there was a pitch invasion, two sendings-off and an enormous brawl involving police, out-of-control spectators and twenty of the twenty-two players. The Boca Juniors goalkeeper was bitten by a police dog called Ron, and Colo fans were so pleased they put up a statue of him. He now has his own Facebook page. The game ended with the overnight imprisonment of two footballers and the Boca coach.

Deciding to kiss and make up they arranged a rematch billed as 'The Friendship Cup' at the Argentine resort of Mar del Plata in February 1992. It all went smoothly until the fiftieth minute when Boca's Antonio Apud was brought down.

Against a background of crowd taunts and personal insults there was a pitch invasion, two sendings-off and an enormous brawl, but this time all twenty-two players joined in.

The Least Successful Substitution

Few substitutes have had more immediate impact upon a game than the Swedish player Andreas Johansson, who came on for Wigan during an away Premier League match against Arsenal in May 2006.

He ran on, fouled an opposition player, got sent off immediately and gave away a penalty, from which Arsenal scored the goal that won not only the match but also the entire championship. He had been on the pitch forty seconds and had not touched the ball. If you had been looking at the programme you would have missed him completely.

The Least Successful Minute's Silence

Congleton Town Football Club gave their oldest supporter, Fred Cope, a terrific send-off in February 1993. In the programme there was a moving notice announcing Mr Cope's death at the age of eighty-five and describing how he had followed Congleton as man and boy.

The players lined up in the centre circle for a minute's silence with their heads bowed. Taking his place as usual on the terrace, Mr Cope asked what was happening and it was not until he was shown the programme that he found out.

'The players were already standing on the pitch when we spotted Fred coming in,' said the Congleton press officer, Chris Phillips. It was hurriedly announced that the minute's silence was now, in fact, going to be for England player and soccer legend Bobby Moore. 'I had a few funny looks on the way in,' Mr Cope said afterwards. The club apologised to Fred and gave him an easy chair for the rest of the game.

QUIZ

The Worst Football Team in Britain

Newspapers are forever running some story or other headlined 'Is This the Worst Team in the Country?' So which is it really?

In one of the most hotly contested areas in our entire field you can choose from any of the following, who have all at various times been acclaimed by their local press as the Worst Football Team in Britain:

1. East Stirlingshire, who came bottom of the lowest league in Scotland for five years until their goalposts were stolen and they came second from bottom.
2. Madron FC of Penzance, who let in 227 goals in a season, including a 55–0 defeat which is the new British all-comers' record. 'Today alone I had calls from three lads who wanted to play with us,' said their manager.
3. The Beaumont Lions from Leicester, who had not won a game for three years. When asked to name their best defender, there was nervous laughter.

4. Siliconix of Swansea, who had not won a game since they were founded three years previously and conceded 142 goals in seven games. Their best results came when they lost 11–1 in a friendly match where the opposition goalkeeper played with a broken leg.

5. Harraby Athletic, who lost their first ever game 19–0 and then went on a ninety-game losing run. The goalkeeper picked the ball out of the net four hundred times in three seasons. In this time they collected just one point and that was because the other team failed to turn up.

6. The Stamford Arms, in the Lowestoft Sunday League, who are the only team to have ended a season with minus two points. They had managed one draw all season, but had three points deducted when they could not even put out a team.

7. Arnos Town Juniors, who lost forty-five games and let in a hugely impressive 530 goals in a single season. 'They have got the heart, but they have not got any football skills or ability,' said their manager, Kevin Cooper. He added that not only was the goalkeeper 'one of our best players', but that the team practised religiously. This is very important. You cannot get results like these without practising.

Answer: None of them.

The worst team in Britain is Northend Thistle on the Isle of Arran, who did not win a game for sixteen years. They last won in 1992, but no one can remember who they beat. Their captain, Matt Milne, said: 'We're from the north end of the island, and the fact is that we've only got about two hun-

dred folk from which to choose a team, and 150 of
them are retired. We have three blokes under forty
in our team, and the rest are knackered after half
an hour.'

In August 2008, watched by Sky Sports cameras,
they ended their record-breaking run by beating
Southend United from the other side of the island
5–4. It was a great moment for the Southenders,
who had themselves once been crowned 'The Worst
Team in Scotland' and are on course to win back
their title. 'Now we are the worst team. It's official,'
said their captain, Eddie Picken. 'We've been a long
time in the doldrums.'

☞ 13 ☜

USING THE LATEST TECHNOLOGY

The Least Successful Use of a Taser Gun
The Worst Photoshop Mistakes
The Least Successful Satnav Use
The Least Efficient Computerisation
The Worst Video Game
The Least Successful Internet Research
The Worst Special Effects
The Most Incomprehensible Instruction Manual
The Least Successful Metal Detection
The Least Successful Beach
The Least Successful Attempt to Make Contact
with Aliens

New Technologies: Their Criminal Application

Making the Most of CCTV
Global Positioning: Advanced Applications
Mobile Phones: A Step in the Right Direction

'If at first you don't succeed, failure may be
your style.'
QUENTIN CRISP

The Least Successful Use of a Taser Gun

Called to a heated domestic dispute in Auckland between a husband and wife and their teenage son in November 2006, a police constable first tried remonstrating with them. When this proved futile, he decided to disable the troublesome husband using his new Taser, an electronic stun gun which he had just been trained to use.

His first shot surprised the cat, which at least brought him under control. The second shot hit the teenager, knocking him to the ground. A third shot also went astray. When the constable tried to remove the spent cartridges, he forgot to wait for the five-second discharge cycle to complete and Tasered himself with fifty thousand volts.

Once he had recovered and reloaded, he fired two further shots, both of which hit the ceiling. At this point he abandoned the Taser gun and took out his pepper spray in another attempt to sort out the husband. This too missed its target and sorted out the couple's twenty-one-year-old daughter, who had just popped in to find out what was happening.

Confronted with a virtuoso, the husband gave himself up.

The Worst Photoshop Mistakes

Google the words 'Photoshop mistakes' and you will be rewarded with millions of results, all cheerfully displaying doctored photographs that have been published after helpful improvement by this excellent device.

The good news is that magazines are now full of models with one leg or a third hand. Indeed, three hands are very common and, let's face it, extremely useful. In swimwear catalogues such hands can nestle upon a model's shoulder offering considerable comfort after a hard day. Even the journalist Max Hastings had a disembodied hand resting proprietorially upon the gate of his attractive country home.

There are headless basketball referees aplenty and rugby referees with no bodies. Thanks to this new process it is now possible for a black model leaping vigorously across a cereal packet to have a white stomach. Even the cosmos can be improved, with two suns setting in a furniture advert.

Celebrities are touched up in particular. President Nicolas Sarkozy of France was given three legs, Brad Pitt and Angelina Jolie's son had two heads and there are photographs of a three-handed Miley Cyrus. Christina Aguilera clutches her dog with her fingers like an intriguing alien claw, Amy Winehouse was seen with ten fingers on one hand and

Penélope Cruz had an elongated neck that must have been at least twelve inches long.

The well-meaning do worry that Photoshopped images will give impressionable young women an unrealistic idea of what they should look like. It is certainly a concern.

The Least Successful Satnav Use

The reigning champion is Necdet Bakimci, a Syrian lorry driver who set out from Antakya in Turkey in 2008 and became more lost under satnav guidance than anyone before or since. Instead of driving to the southernmost tip of Spain, he ended up a record 1,600 miles adrift before driving his thirty-two-ton lorry with a cargo of luxury cars into a nature reserve at Gibraltar Point near Skegness. A birdwatcher, who was asked for directions to Coral Road, Gibraltar, said that the driver 'didn't seem too upset'.

The Least Efficient Computerisation

In 1993 the French railways (SNCF) decided to buy Socrates, a stunning new computer system that promised to cope with the increase in ticket reservations from forty million to an expected 140 million in a decade. Pioneering cheaper rail travel, this innovative computer was soon charging zero francs for a ticket from Paris to Frankfurt. It also made full use of the rail network, routinely sending empty trains across France.

In travel agencies they had to figure out the complex destination code (01B1NN! 460 'FIN') and then input journey-specific reservation formulae such as 'EW\$FC AS QICS 45'. The marvellous thing was that if only one digit or symbol was incorrectly entered then the passengers would be sent to discover new and exciting parts of France. Obviously computers, due to their chips and wiring, have greater innate potential than we Homo Sapiens will ever have, but there is still a crucial role for us to play.

The Worst Video Game

In a highly competitive market, *ET: The Extra Terrestrial* has been recommended as the worst game of all time by *PC World*, *Electronic Gaming Monthly* and *FHM* magazines. It was an enthralling divertissement in which the much-loved film alien had to jump into pits that looked like potties and find parts of his telephone. To get him out you had to stretch his neck until he rose very, very, very slowly to the top. There you were given a nanosecond to stop stretching or he would fall to the bottom again. You could get really skilful at it after twenty goes.

Atari manufactured five million games car-tridges. 'Nearly all of them came back,' according to the company's chief executive officer. It got to a point where children refused to take them for free. Eventually, Atari dumped the whole lot in a landfill site in New Mexico and covered them with cement.

The Least Successful Internet Research

The internet is an exciting research tool and the Greek football team Aris Thessaloniki took full advantage of it when preparing for a Europa League game in February 2011 against Manchester City, the richest football club in the world.

Searching the World Wide Web for a photograph of City's expensive squad to put in the official pro-gramme, the editorial team located a *Where's Wally?* spoof picture and did not realise the difference.

With its billionaire owner, the Manchester club routinely buys up batches of superstar footballers. Thus the photo showed a satirically doctored squad of seventy-seven players instead of the legally per-mitted twenty-five. Sitting in seven enormous rows, the swollen gathering included eight world-famous goalkeepers and all the greatest players on the planet – from Chelsea's Drogba to Real Madrid's Kaká. Also present was Wally from the popular British children's book, whose habit is to lurk in large crowds wearing his characteristic red-and-white hooped jumper so that the sharp-eyed young can have hours of fun finding him. (He was seated in row three, next to Barcelona's Ibrahimovic.)

The Worst Special Effects

Released in 1953, *Robot Monster* was immediately hailed by critics as 'certainly among the finest terrible movies ever made', but this is almost entirely due to its unbeatable array of special effects.

The central robot character, which was acclaimed as 'the most ridiculous monster in screen history' in the 1978 Golden Turkey awards, was an actor in a gorilla costume and a diver's helmet. The whole magnificent thing was topped off with specially glued antennae like splayed rabbit ears.

The story tells of two scientists, who are never seen, but who nonetheless escape in a rocket to a space platform. Fortunately, we are allowed to see the platform, which is a toy jet plane with a sparkler attached. When it blows up you can see the stick and a gloved hand holding it.

Mesmerising also is the lavish provision of bubbles. So many films lack bubbles to any adequate degree or even at all, but this is not a charge you could ever make against *Robot Monster*.

The film's sponsor was N. A. Fisher Chemical Products Ltd, who just happened to make an 'Automatic Billion Bubble Machine' that gets its own credit at the end. This fine contraption appears at regular intervals and emits a profusion of bubbles for reasons that are wisely never explained.

The Most Incomprehensible
Instruction Manual

The ever watchful journal of the Institute of Scientific and Technical Communicators has rightly drawn attention to the following enigmatic direction taken from an aircraft electronics manual:

The internal guidance system uses deviations to generate corrective commands to fly the aircraft from a position where it is to a position where it isn't. The aircraft arrives at the position where it wasn't, thus, the position where it was is the position where it isn't. In the event that the position where it is now is not the same as the position where it originally wasn't, the system will acquire a variation (variations are caused by external factors and discussion of these factors is beyond the scope of this simple explanation).

The Least Successful Metal Detection

A top-notch fireman was employed in July 1986 to locate water hydrants that had been inadvertently covered by tarmac on roads in Bath. Using a special metal detector, he identified one almost immediately, but when a hole was dug nothing could be found. A tireless public servant, he had caused seven enormous holes to be dug in the same road, all in the wrong places, when he realised that his steel toe caps were activating the device.

The Least Successful Beach

We humans exploit Mother Nature for our own needs. It is always take, take, take with us; everywhere except Burnham upon Crouch, which alone seems willing to give something back.

Seeing the need for a visitor attraction in 1994, their district council instructed the National Rivers Authority to create a man-made pleasure beach at West Quay on the estuary. The whole thing was held in place by state-of-the-art technology, involving steel groynes.

All three hundred tons of sand was washed out to sea in the very first tide. 'They said this would not happen,' observed the mayor of Burnham.

The Least Successful Attempt to Make Contact with Aliens

At long last scientists had contacted an alien. For years the SETI Institute – Search for Extraterrestrial Intelligence – had been scouring eight hundred stars and planets for signs of life elsewhere in the galaxy. Then suddenly at their outback telescope station in Australia researchers picked up a signal.

'It was pretty loud,' said Dr Peter Backus.

At first they could not believe it, but then it started happening every night at the same time. ET was trying to get in touch. Joy was unbounded. Here at last was evidence of new life and new civilisations Out There.

On 16 January 1996 Dr Backus addressed the American Astronomical Society in Texas on this breakthrough discovery. 'It was a microwave oven in the kitchen,' he said. 'We thought it was odd that this only happened at mealtimes.'

NEW TECHNOLOGIES: THEIR CRIMINAL APPLICATION

Making the Most of CCTV

In April 1993 Steve Driscoll entered the Sony Centre in Cardiff with the intention of stealing a camcorder. Eyeing up a wall display, he spotted the one he wanted, not realising it was the shop's CCTV camera.

He waited until the shop was really busy, which was a nice touch, and then repeatedly jumped to reach it in front of an appreciative and growing crowd. 'He was staring straight into the lens,' said Dean Clark, the store's manager. 'It was the perfect shot of him, better than a passport photo. He might as well have posed for a picture and sent it to the police before he committed the crime.'

Global Positioning: Advanced Applications

Kurt Husfeldt was amazed when police knocked on his door as soon as he got back from committing a crime in January 2007. 'He was astonished that we had been able to track him down so quickly,' said a spokesman for Suffolk County police.

He had just broken into the Babylon public works warehouse in Lindenhurst, New York, and stolen a box full of what he thought were mobile phones. In fact, they were fourteen Global Positioning Systems intended to help police locate the whereabouts of snowploughs lost in drifts. When he got home Mr Husfeldt helpfully powered one up to see how it worked. The police tapped into their GPS system and drove straight over.

Mobile Phones: A Step in the Right Direction

In September 2001 a thief in Hastings had stolen a handbag and run a short distance when a mobile phone rang inside it. The model of politeness, he stopped running and not only answered it immediately, but also gave his location to PC Jason Tuck on the other end of the line.

'Look,' said PC Tuck, 'keep the money, but can you leave the bag and the mobile somewhere?'

'I'll leave it here,' said the thief. When the policeman asked where 'here' was, he replied, 'Outside the cinema.'

'You're nicked,' said PC Tuck, who was now standing behind him.

☞ 14 ☜

IT'S HAPPENING RIGHT HERE, RIGHT NOW

The Worst Theme Park
The Least Successful Drugs Raid
The Worst TV Results Announcement
The Least Successful Book Launch
The Worst Busker
The Art of Getting Lost
The Most Boring Conference
The Most Badly Timed Police Raid
The Worst Subtitles for the Hearing Impaired
The Worst Commonwealth Games

'Failure is authentic, and because it's authentic, it's real and genuine, and because of that, it's a pure state of being.'

DOUGLAS COUPLAND

The Worst Theme Park

At long last a theme park worth visiting. Those who tire of identical days out at corporate theme parks were rewarded in 2010 when Lapland New Forest opened near Bournemouth.

It promised 'a winter wonderland' replete with animal attractions, an ice rink, snow-covered log cabins, a nativity scene, a 'magical tunnel of light', a polar bear and the pledge that every visitor would be escorted to Santa's grotto by Seamus the Elf. 'The attention to detail in our theme park will really wow you,' said the publicity leaflet. It certainly did.

A magical vista opened up before amazed visitors. The venue 'looked like a war zone', they said. The ice rink was two large puddles because the generator had malfunctioned. The magical tunnel was a few fairy lights dangling from trees covered with artificial snow. The polar bear was plastic. The nativity was an 'amateurishly painted' billboard with sandy mountains, three camels and a star. The log cabins were green garden sheds. The animal attractions were a handful of reindeer, some 'thin-looking huskies chained up in a pen yapping' and several chickens. And there was no sign of Seamus the Elf. One child had to be consoled when he found Father Christmas smoking a cigarette outside the grotto.

In other theme parks people wander round like sedated zombies without real audience involvement or reaction, but not here. In no time visitors had formed into a vibrant and gesticulating crowd outside the manager's officer. Santa was attacked and one of the elves got smacked and pushed into a pram.

A lot of us would pay good money to see this feast of entertainment, but it was closed down after only one week because they were charging an outrageous £30 to get in. Very little in this life is worth paying £30 for, not even this.

The Least Successful Drugs Raid

Ever vigilant in the fight against drugs, Bradford police were quick to react when a force helicopter picked up a 'hotspot' at Pam Hardcastle's house in Bradford. In January 2011 the squad raced to the site of this suspected cannabis farm. Six officers rushed out with a battering ram while others scoured the district to find Ms Hardcastle.

The hotspot turned out to be a garage where they found a heater and two pet guinea pigs belonging to her ten-year-old son, Jack. 'When I opened it up and they saw Simon and Kenny, they didn't say anything,' Ms Hardcastle said. 'They were in the garage two seconds and they left.'

Guinea pigs are sarcastic animals and well able to run a drugs cartel, but it is often difficult to pin anything on them.

The Worst TV Results Announcement

Normally in the final of *Australia's Next Top Model* only one person gets the chance to be a wonderful loser admired by all for her grace and dignity in defeat. The 2010 series changed all that and expanded what is possible in talent shows of this kind.

In the final programme the contestants had been whittled down to the last two and Australia held its breath. Would Kelsey or Amanda win the fabled catwalk contract?

'And the winner is . . .' said the presenter, Sarah Murdoch. There followed the usual pause that was long enough to make tea, visit Mum and redecorate the landing in a blue-wash frottage. 'It's you, Kelsey.'

The audience went wild. All eyes were on the loser.

'I want to say thank you to the runner-up, who has been amazing,' Kelsey said to Amanda. 'I mean, she's incredible, isn't she?'

'Thank you so much,' said Amanda, who was adopting an expression of impossibly patient forbearance and even-tempered stoicism.

Kelsey began the usual catalogue of thanks to all and sundry. Then there was sudden drama. Listening to the producer through her earpiece, Ms Murdoch grew twitchy. 'Oh, my God, I don't know what to say right now. I'm feeling a bit sick about this.'

The audience fell silent.

'I'm so sorry about this. Oh, my God.' Ms Murdoch put her hand over her mouth. 'It's Amanda. I'm so sorry. It was fed to me wrong.'

'It's fine. Don't worry,' said Kelsey, who saw her chance, grabbed centre stage and basked in the spotlight of gracious defeat. 'It's okay. It's an honest mistake. It's fine.' She was magnificent. Frankly, it was difficult to choose between them.

The Least Successful Book Launch

In April 2010 Penguin Australia destroyed seven thousand copies of *The Pasta Bible* after a misprint told readers to use 'salt and freshly ground black people' in a recipe for tagliatelle, sardines and prosciutto when it should have said 'black pepper'. Dwarfing this achievement only six months later, HarperCollins published eighty thousand copies not of Jonathan Franzen's new novel, *Freedom*, in its finished form but of an earlier, fresher and more spontaneous first draft.

According to its author, the book was adorned with 'hundreds of mistakes at the level of words, sentence and fact' as well as 'small but significant changes to the characterisations of Jessica and Lalitha'.

A '*Freedom* Recall Hotline' was set up inviting readers to exchange their blunder-emblazoned books for the corrected version. Unsurprisingly, a great number decided to keep their original purchase. A spokesman for Waterstone's bookshop said they had not yet received a single complaint about the faulty copies. Indeed, interest in buying the error-bedazzled version rocketed following news about the mistakes. 'I wouldn't be surprised if a lot of people started popping in to pick one up,' he said.

Franzen's previous bestseller was entitled *The Corrections.*

The Worst Busker

Hailed as Britain's most tuneless busker in December 2010, Bryan Bryn starts with the God-given, natural advantage of being tone-deaf, but he brings so much more than that to his work.

Mr Bryn gained early recognition: 'He should stop trying to entertain the public,' critics said. Like Vincent Van Gogh, he was not immediately understood.

Twice a week he travels from his home in Ely, Cambridgeshire, to the bright lights of Bury St Edmunds to wow them with his sea shanties.

Equipped with deaf aids in not one but both ears, he takes up his regular spot near the market and accompanies himself with a flexible saw. 'If he's not the worst busker in the world he is very close to it,' said Paul Kempson, a resident of Bury St Edmunds. 'Everything he sings sounds exactly the same and you can never make out any of the songs.'

In fact, he is not the worst ever. This honour falls to the late great Mushroom Mick, who won this coveted title in a *News of the World* poll after the MP for Bath accused him of scaring tourists away from the city centre with his 'nasal, tuneless warbling'. After enchanting Bath and later Totnes, he relocated to Glastonbury, where he was often to be heard outside the NatWest bank singing 'All along the Watchtower'. The great man always ranked himself, musically speaking, alongside the Sex Pistols.

The Art of Getting Lost

In November 2010 John Marsden left his home in Bolton at eight thirty in the morning intending to spend a fortnight in a caravan near Rhyl in north Wales, a journey that should have taken an hour and a half, tops. Travelling in his Vauxhall Cavalier, he was armed with what he described as 'a book of maps'.

Stopped near Bangor fourteen hours later, having driven six and a half miles the wrong way down a dual carriageway, Mr Marsden said he was a member of the Institute of Advanced Motorists and the previous year he had not only driven back from Kent without incident but also around the Greek island of Kos.

Describing his journey as 'a blur', he said he had gone backwards and forwards asking directions, but 'no one seemed to agree'.

It takes a lot of advanced driving skills to master a journey like this and he decided to retire at the top. 'I have a lovely electric scooter. In future I'm going to drive that. It only does eight miles an hour.' There is a lot of possibility here. This is not the end, but a new beginning.

The Most Boring Conference

Held in December 2011 at the Dominion Theatre in London, the Boring Conference was a sell-out. The organiser, James Ward, opened the proceedings with a talk on his tie collection, which he discussed at some length.

He noted that as of June 2010, he owned fifty-five ties and 45.5 per cent of them were a single colour. By December, his tie collection had jumped by 36 per cent, although the share of single-colour ties fell by 1.5 per cent. 'Ties are getting slightly more colourful,' he noted.

This was followed by a tutored milk tasting in

which a connoisseur swirled, sniffed and sipped five different milks in wine glasses, commenting on each one's flavour, finish and ideal food pairing.

One eagerly awaited talk was given by Peter Fletcher, who had logged his every sneeze since 2007. With the help of graphs and charts, Mr Fletcher disclosed that he had sneezed 2,267 times in the past 1,249 days. 'I've even sneezed when recording a sneeze,' he said.

After a much-needed break, a raffle was held. The winners received a DVD called *Helvetica*, a 2007 documentary about typographical fonts.

The Most Badly Timed Police Raid

Leading from the front, the newly appointed Commissioner of the Metropolitan Police, Sir Paul Stephenson, got off to a cracking start in March 2009. He personally led an elite force of top officers in an early-morning raid to catch the boss of a notorious burglary gang.

In this high-profile operation, eighty police and detectives, including Sir Paul, swooped on addresses in Surrey and south London. Some of the task force were equipped with Taser guns. A Met helicopter hovered overhead as officers using a battering ram broke down the head honcho's front door, which probably needed to come off anyway.

Only when they got inside did Sir Paul learn that the ringleader was not there. He was already in prison, having been arrested five hours earlier by the local constabulary, as had nine members of his gang. 'It was a very professional operation,' Sir Paul said.

The Worst Subtitles for the Hearing Impaired

Computer voice recognition has proved the most wonderful boon for subtitling of TV programmes. Before this great onward leap of technology the BBC employed stenographers typing words phonetically as they were spoken.

Now computers recognise the words. This is much better, particularly as they often use words that sound similar to the ones actually spoken, but with excitingly different meanings.

During the Queen Mother's funeral in 2002, for example, the solemn words 'We will now have a moment's silence for the Queen Mother' became 'We will now have a moment's violence for the Queen Mother.'

In January 2011, during an item about breeding pigs on a BBC breakfast show, a roving reporter explained to the studio presenter that pigs 'love to nibble anything that comes into the shed, like our wellies'.

Spotting an opportunity, the computer heard this as pigs 'love to nibble anything that comes into the shed, like our willies'.

The second this subtitling appeared, with its crucial new insight into pig psychology, the internet was ablaze. The actual pig report, by contrast, was completely forgotten.

The Worst Commonwealth Games

Normally, getting out of games involves arranging a sick note from the doctor, which can be very time-consuming. Organisers of the 2010 Commonwealth Games in Delhi, however, laid on special provisions to streamline the whole process.

First, a bridge from the athletes' car park collapsed, as did the scoreboard at the stadium and the ceiling in the weightlifting arena. Amidst fears of rising flood water, the athletes' village was condemned by team officials as unfit for human occupation because the toilets were blocked.

Next a poisonous snake was found in the tennis court, mosquitoes brought the prospect of dengue fever, paw prints were found all over the athletes' beds and swimmers got instant Delhi belly.

Specially trained black-faced langurs, which are highly intelligent primates, were brought in to protect athletes and visitors from attack by the common Indian bonnet monkey. This was shortly before the bus drivers' strike and technical problems with the Metro.

With a week to go, many athletes were told that it was up to them individually whether they attended or not. Getting out of games has never been easier.

15

NO SMOKE WITHOUT FIRE: STORIES I FAILED TO PIN DOWN

The Worst Weather Forecast
The Least Successful Pageant
The Worst Referee
The Worst Pub Bore
The Least Successful Village Bank Robbery
The Least Successful Police Poster
The Least Successful Demonstration
The Least Successful Exhibition
The Worst Angler
The Worst Post-Office Raid
The Least Successful Witchcraft
The Worst Golf Shot

'As I said, there is nothing wrong with failing.'
HENRY KRAVIS, AMERICAN FINANCIER

There comes a point when we all have a clear duty to give up. I reached that point while trying to pin down the following stories, all of which eluded research and verification.

The Worst Weather Forecast

In the 1990s a Delhi TV news programme abandoned its nightly forecast because the weatherman kept getting it wrong. One night he told viewers to keep their woollen underwear on and the next day the temperature was 102 degrees. The following night he promised more sunshine and there were four inches of snow.

Eventually he started blubbing in the middle of the bulletin while explaining that these were freak weather conditions for April. The TV channel faded him out.

Explaining the decision to drop the forecast, a newsreader said, 'The weather has become too complicated, but we hope to have the forecast back in May as it is always blazing hot so he should be able to cope.'

The Least Successful Pageant

Plans to have a pageant celebrating the main historical events at a town in Essex were called off when it was discovered that there weren't any. After six months of investigation by a specially commissioned pageant coordinator it emerged that the only notable events in the town's eight-hundred-year history were the development of a local branch line in Victorian times and a minor uprising in the Peasants' Revolt of 1381 that had no lasting significance. Neither was thought sufficiently interesting to justify a pageant.

Other more excitable places are always having pageants about the noisy and often upsetting events that have pockmarked their history. In this blissfully restful town, by contrast, the committee suggested a community parade with a local belly-dancing troupe very much to the fore in an Arabian Nights tableau, which was vastly more attractive.

The Worst Referee

The most important referee in the history of association football sent himself off because he was so awful.

Obviously in a decisive mood, he had already sent off the wrong player in a Hampshire senior cup match between two Bournemouth teams. As the disgraced striker, Wayne Pigford, left the pitch his honest teammate ran over to the ref and said that it was he himself personally who had kicked six bells out of the opposition goalie and not Mr Pigford in the slightest.

Taking full control of the situation, the referee stunned spectators when he pulled out a red card, showed it to himself and left the pitch ten minutes before half-time. To his credit he did not show any of the shirty dissent or eye-rolling disbelief that can so easily disfigure such occasions.

'I have never seen anything like it in all my footballing days,' a player said. 'As he walked towards the tunnel, we all thought he was going to talk to the linesman, but he just kept on going.'

The Worst Pub Bore

Effortlessly swatting aside 260 red-hot rivals, a retired seaman won the Pub Bore of the Year contest organised in 1994 by a brewery industry magazine. 'Some seriously boring people were nominated,' said the organiser, 'but he stood head and shoulders above the rest.'

Although confronted by a man from Ipswich who could talk in exhaustive detail about his conservatory extension, our chap's supporters from Hayle in Cornwall remained confident. 'It had to be him. He drones on and on. It's incessant,' said the barmaid at his local, throwing down the gauntlet.

Selfless with his time and expertise, this cracking performer is at his best on the subject of local bus timetables, unreliable batteries for his hearing aid and his time in the Royal Marines. He won the contest by a landslide vote after a tour-de-force address confronting head-on the lack of bus shelters in Hayle.

The Least Successful Village Bank Robbery

In 1987 a village branch of Barclays saw a bank robbery for connoisseurs. One busy lunchtime a long queue was waiting when all at once a pensioner ducked under the rail, stuck a gun over the counter and demanded the money in the cash drawer.

The bank teller was just going to follow his manager's instruction to hand over some money and press the alarm bell when a second pensioner came up behind the first one, grabbed him by the scruff of the neck and, shouting 'Queue jumper,' marched him out of the bank and into the street. 'It was quite a relief,' the bank teller said afterwards.

The Least Successful Police Poster

In January 1988 the police department of the Australian railway system launched a new poster showing what they considered to be a potential fare dodger approaching the barrier at Calvary station. It was withdrawn when it was discovered that the person on the photograph was the mayor.

The Least Successful Demonstration

In 2001 a South African inventor launched his revolutionary new device, a groin protection box for cricketers. Appearing at a press conference, he said that it was equipped with a system of coiled springs that would lessen the impact of a direct hit from a hard, fast-travelling cricket ball.

Wearing only a jockstrap containing the box to provide a photo opportunity, he said, 'As you can see, it fits snugly over the groin,' adding that he had tested it by hitting himself in the groin with a cricket bat. He was now ready to face public scrutiny and invited his audience to throw cricket balls at him.

Wincing audibly as he was carried off to hospital only a few minutes later, he said there would now be a short delay for further research and development before the product went into full-scale commercial production.

The Least Successful Exhibition

Thrilled to see the local state governor arriving in a hovercraft to inaugurate a Canadian sandcastle competition, an enthusiastic crowd surged forward on the beach and knocked down most of the exhibits.

Among those destroyed beyond recognition was a model of the Canadian parliament building which had taken twenty-seven hours to construct. The winner of the competition was the only exhibit left completely intact: a model of the White Rock lunatic asylum.

'We had no idea the governor was so popular,' said the competition organiser.

The Worst Angler

In the world of fishing one man stands head and shoulders above all others. In forty years of enthusiastic angling he did not catch a single fish. Keen as mustard, he was in countless competitions and would think nothing of travelling long distances to find a new and copiously stocked fishing lake. He was hooked even if nothing else was.

For four decades he savoured the fresh air, the weather, the rippling stream, the occasional flash of fin in the reeds and the very occasional struggle with something on the end of his line, leaving fish to swim unhindered in the rivers of Britain.

At the age of seventy this angler, said to be a wood turner from Staffordshire called Mr Golder, travelled to a fishing complex in Devon when he caught a six-pound carp and spoiled everything.

The Worst Post-Office Raid

March 1988. The sub-postmaster had just finished serving some customers when a man walked into his Yorkshire post office, took a shotgun from under his coat and demanded money. Before anything else could happen, another man walked in and said to the gunman: 'Hello, Russell. What are you doing here?'

The chap replied: 'Keep quiet and stay where you are, Henry Jones,' and pointed the shotgun in his direction, whereupon Mr Jones, as he turned out to be, fainted.

Shouting 'You have ruined everything,' the man threw down the shotgun and ran off.

The Least Successful Witchcraft

A pre-eminent South African witch-doctor offered a specialist service freeing people in court cases. In May 1994 three of his clients were appearing in Port Elizabeth charged with robbery when our man arrived to sort things out.

Approaching the court with two chickens, he immediately started casting spells, chanting and waving poultry at the building. Officials gazed on in awe as the chickens escaped and he proceeded to drink brown liquid containing animal entrails before spitting the foul-smelling mixture on the court doors.

He then entered the court flinging some powder and entrails at the judge's bench and two witnesses whom he was apparently hired to jinx.

His traditional ritual was brought to a halt when court officers arrested him. The judge sentenced our hero's clients to one hundred years between them, which everyone thought harsh, and the chickens were confiscated.

The Worst Golf Shot

In October 1987 Matthieu Boya popped out during his lunch break for some golf practice next to an air base in the African state of Benin.

Slicing his shot to perfection, he drove the ball over the fence and into a passing bird, which coughed, squawked and plummeted towards the runway, smashing into the windscreen of a plane about to take off and alarming the pilot, who slammed on his brakes and skidded, plunging into Benin's four (and only) military jets.

With a single golf stroke this important athlete had wiped out his country's entire air force.

THE ART OF BEING WRONG

'There is no reason anyone would want a computer in their home.' Ken Olsen, Digital Equipment Corp., 1977.

'Computers in the future may weigh no more than 1.5 tons.' *Popular Mechanics*, forecasting the relentless march of science in 1949.

'This "telephone" has too many shortcomings to be seriously considered as a means of communication. The device is inherently of no value to us.' Western Union memo, 1876.

'The Americans have need of the telephone, but we do not. We have plenty of messenger boys.' Sir William Preece, British Post Office, 1876.

'The wireless music box has no imaginable commercial value. Who would pay for a message sent to nobody in particular?' David Sarnoff's associates in response to his urgings in the 1920s, as founder of NBC, for investment in the radio.

'While theoretically and technically television may be feasible, commercially and financially it is an impossibility.' Lee DeForest, inventor.

'Who the hell wants to hear actors talk?' H. M. Warner, Warner Brothers, 1927, on the talking motion picture.

'It will be years – not in my time – before a woman will become prime minister.' Margaret Thatcher, 26 October 1969.

'There is not the slightest indication that nuclear energy will ever be obtainable. It would mean that the atom would have to be shattered at will.' Albert Einstein, 1932.

'Louis Pasteur's theory of germs is ridiculous fiction.' Pierre Pachet, professor of physiology at Toulouse, 1872.

'The abdomen, the chest and the brain will forever be shut from the intrusion of the wise and humane surgeon.' Sir John Eric Erichsen, British surgeon (appointed Surgeon-Extraordinary to Queen Victoria, 1873).

'Stocks have reached what looks like a permanently high plateau.' Professor Irving Fisher, Yale University, 1929, shortly before the Wall Street Crash.

'So we went to Atari and said, "Hey, we've got this amazing thing, even built with some of your parts, and what do you think about funding us? Or we'll give it to you. We just want to do it. Pay our salary, we'll come work for you." And they said, "No." So then we went to Hewlett-Packard, and they said, "Hey, we don't need you. You haven't got through college yet."' Steve Jobs, founder of Apple Computer Inc., on attempts to get Atari and Hewlett-Packard interested in his and Steve Wozniak's personal computer.

'The bomb will never go off. I speak as an expert in explosives.' Admiral William Leahy, on the US atomic bomb project.

'This fellow Charles Lindbergh will never make it. He's doomed.' Harry Guggenheim, millionaire aviation enthusiast, shortly before Lindbergh completed his successful solo flight across the Atlantic.

'It will be gone by June.' *Variety* magazine passing judgement on rock 'n' roll in 1955.

'The Beatles are not merely awful – I would consider it sacrilegious to say anything less than that they are God-awful. They are so unbelievably horrible, so appallingly unmusical, so dogmatically insensitive to the magic of the art, that they qualify as crowned heads of anti-music, even as the impostor popes went down in history as "anti-popes".' William F. Buckley, journalist, 1964.

'The singer will have to go; the BBC won't like him.' The Rolling Stones' first manager, Eric Easton, to his partner after watching Mick Jagger perform.

'The horse is here to stay but the automobile is only a novelty – a fact.' The president of Michigan Savings Bank, advising Henry Ford's lawyer not to invest in the Ford Motor Company in 1903.

'Television won't last because people will soon get tired of staring at a plywood box every night.' Darryl Zanuck, movie producer, 20th Century Fox, 1946.

'Nuclear-powered vacuum cleaners will probably be a reality in ten years.' Alex Lewyt, president of the Lewyt Corp vacuum-cleaner company, in the *New York Times*, 1955.

'The biggest no talent I ever worked with.' Decca boss rejecting Buddy Holly.

'I give the Rolling Stones about another two years.' Mick Jagger in 1964.

'Can't act. Can't sing. Slightly bald. Can dance a little.' Film company's verdict on Fred Astaire's 1928 screen test.

'You have a chip on your tooth, your Adam's apple sticks out too far and you talk too slow.' Film executive rejecting Clint Eastwood in 1959.

'Reagan doesn't have the presidential look.' Producer rejecting Ronald Reagan for the role of president in a 1964 film.

'You ought to go back to driving a truck.' Concert manager firing Elvis Presley in 1954.

'Forget it. No civil war picture ever made a nickel.' MGM executive advising against investing in *Gone with the Wind.*

'You'd better learn secretarial skills or else get married.' Modelling agency rejecting Marilyn Monroe in 1944.

'That rainbow song is no good. Take it out.' MGM memo after the initial showing of *The Wizard of Oz.*

'We are willing to return the manuscript.' Publisher rejecting Jane Austen's novel *Northanger Abbey.*

'Pull the other one.' Careers adviser at Gosforth High School when the young Alan Shearer said he wanted to be a professional footballer. Shearer won sixty-three caps for England and set the world-record transfer fee in 1996.

'You will never get anywhere playing that kind of stuff.' The same careers adviser at Gosforth High School to Mark Knopfler, who went on to earn £50 million from worldwide hits with Dire Straits.

'I watched agape with admiration while he strolled around the stage with every appearance of knowing where he was going, and I burst into spontaneous applause as he strode down to *within a foot of the orchestra pit* without the least sign of fear. By the end of his act I was misty with tears at the thought of his courage.' Theatre critic Kenneth Tynan, reviewing the 1960s singer Frank Ifield at the London Palladium in the mistaken belief that he was blind.

EPILOGUE

Interviewer: 'Why did you make a film about the worst footballer in Brazil, Mauro Shampoo, and not about the best, Pelé or Ronaldo?'

Leonardo Cunha Lima: 'Mauro's story had something that I find particularly interesting – a sense of the irony of life. This is a film about a man who turns the otherwise catastrophic fact of his failure into a positive thing. He achieved his goal in a completely unexpected upside-down way.

'After all, most Brazilians will become Mauro Shampoos, and only a few will ever see the glories of Ronaldo. So Mauro is the perfect role model for failing with dignity and pride, but still to succeed in those things that really matter in life: a loving family, his own business and the respect of his community. What more could a man wish for?

'There is an idealist in me who sees the perpetuation of this myth of the winner in a country of millions of losers as a small ethical crime.'

Kicking and Screening Film Festival, New York, 2010

'You can't blame me for hating success when it changes all the things I love best.'
NOEL COWARD, *Design for Living*

'Failure has gone to his head.'
WILSON MIZNER

ACKNOWLEDGEMENTS

I would like to thank Herdis Lien, curator at the Svalbard Museum, for her expertise on unsuccessful polar expeditions; Maria Tønnesen for translating Norwegian newspapers; Ken McCoy, alias Prof. Albert Crapper, for admitting everything; Jennifer Hall for services to horticulture and sending details of the Beadnell Alternative Flower Show; Jeremy Willis for confirming that a helicopter with a winch was necessary after the school talk; Michael Ford and his website www.bigredbook.info for information on Eamonn Andrews; that master of disguise, PC Dean Cunnington, who wants it made clear that it was early in the morning and he got into the building eventually; the Office of the Historian of the House of Representatives, Washington; and the Rare Breeds Centre, Ashford, Kent. I would like to thank Robin Halstead, Jason Hazeley, Alex Morris and Joel Morris for permission to quote from p. 119 of *Bollocks To Alton Towers* and pp. 142 and 207 of *Far From the Sodding Crowd*, published by Michael Joseph and reproduced by Penguin Books Ltd © Robin Halstead, Jason Hazeley, Alex Morris and Joel Morris.

I would also like to thank Bill Addis for his critical reading of the manuscript and many helpful suggestions; my son Nicholas for his conscientious research; my daughter Eleanor for her detailed thoughts on the first draft; my son Jonathan for making good jokes usually at my expense; and my wife Siân for absolutely everything, not least endlessly trailing to the British Library, organising my chaotic filing system, feeding me, tracking down heroes of our time, even owl experts and a disguised policeman (see above), and reading at length not only about the unfolding saga of the Eurovision Song Contest, but also about the history of rugby league in Liverpool, which is beyond the call of duty.

Finally, I would like to thank everyone mentioned in this book because in our success-crazed times they shine out as beacons of sanity and good humour.